THE JUDO HANDBOOK

FROM BEGINNER TO BLACK BELT

First published in Great Britain in 1989
by Ward Lock Limited, 8 Clifford Street
London W1X 1RB, an Egmont Company

This edition published in 1989 by Gallery Books,
an imprint of W.H. Smith Publishers, Inc.,
112 Madison Avenue, New York, New York 10016

Japanese characters on pages 4–5 by Eric George
Illustrations by Mark Iley
Designed by David Robinson
Photographs by Derek Bannister, D.B. Studios
Photograph on page 132 by Ernest Singleton
Typeset by Lasertext Ltd
Printed and bound in Great Britain by
Hazell, Watson & Viney Ltd,
Members of the BPCC Group, Aylesbury, Bucks

ISBN 0-8317-5274-2

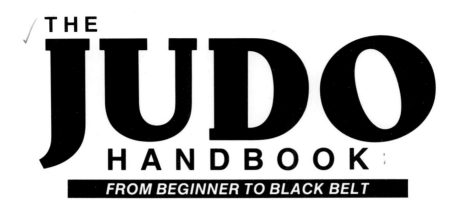

THE JUDO HANDBOOK

FROM BEGINNER TO BLACK BELT

BRIAN CAFFARY
WITH DESMOND MARWOOD

GALLERY BOOKS
An Imprint of W. H. Smith Publishers Inc.
112 Madison Avenue
New York City 10016

CONTENTS

NAGE-WAZA (throwing techniques)   27

TACHI-WAZA (standing techniques)
TE-WAZA (hand techniques)

KOSHI-WAZA (hip techniques)

ASHI-WAZA (foot and leg techniques)

SUTEMI-WAZA (sacrifice techniques)

MA-SUTEMI-WAZA (rear sacrifice techniques)

横捨身技

YOKO-SUTEMI-WAZA (*side sacrifice techniques*)

固技

KATAME-WAZA (*groundwork techniques*) 110

OSAE-KOMI-WAZA (*hold-down techniques*)

KANSETSU-WAZA (*arm-locks*) 117

絞技

SHIME-WAZA (*strangle techniques*) 123

Robin Otani Go-Dan 大谷昌文

A beginner in Judo must realize that progress will be slow, but that any rewards are proportionally deep and profoundly satisfying for every tangible achievement. It is a strenuous sport in which fitness can be built up progressively in step with the accumulation of particular skills. It is not a sport recommended for the ill-disciplined or the faint-hearted, or for those seeking a martial art form in which they hope to achieve push-button results or easy proficiency.

Judo makes demands upon the player's mind and body. However, any who feel that they can become expert in the art of Judo through mental knowledge or physical effort alone are sadly misguided. An over-emphasis on either prohibits the development of an essential balance between the two.

Additionally, the mental disciplines of Judo result in the judoka acquiring a confidence and peace of mind which he or she can very often apply to the handling of life's problems in general. When that state is realized, the full and proper philosophy of Judo has been learned and understood.

Of course, my own introduction to Judo was nurtured by the family environment in which I was born and grew up. I was fortunate to be the son of Masutaro Otani, one of the great founders of the sport of Judo in Britain. My father came from a village about 30 km from Nagasaki. Situated on Kyushu, the southern island of Japan, the region was renowned for having produced some of the toughest Samurai. My father's Japanese accent was apparently as difficult to understand as a broad-tongued Scot is to a southerner. He was the third eldest son among eight brothers and sisters. His father was head of the family group. Under an edict from the Emperor of Japan, the family was trying to adjust to becoming farmers after being of the Samurai class.

My father started Kendo, then compulsory at school, when only six years old but, because he was bullied by an older boy, he switched to Judo (which was the alternative choice) to protect himself. At the age of fifteen he overheard a fierce family row during which some relatives attacked my grandfather in a dispute over financial matters. Overcome by emotion, my father took up the family sword and chased the relatives from his father's house. Then, in shame, he ran away to sea. He eventually landed in Liverpool in the 1920s and remained in England until his death in 1977.

The realization that my father had a special role in life did not come to me suddenly. From my earliest recollection, he returned from a full day's work and went straight out to Judo every evening. Every other weekend he would be away on a Judo course, and later my brother Billy and I would often accompany him.

Many different Judo people would come to our house and their reverence and deep respect for my father was apparent to me even as a young child. I recall my father reprimanding Judo people on many occasions for what seemed trivialities to me, but I realized later that he expected the best from everybody. In all, I never knew him to lie or be dishonest in any way or to put himself before others. His character was true and straight, displaying a wonderful kindness to everyone around him. I could never have wished for a finer example to try to follow in life.

In 1957, at the age of thirteen, I decided to compete in Judo against senior judoka. My father was then fifty-eight years old and, while I had often seen him in action before that time, it was too late for me to experience his technique as it had been during his prime. Nevertheless, the greatness of his ability was still apparent.

Brian Caffary is a senior grade (4th Dan), and I greatly welcome his efforts in producing the book and feel sure it will make a real contribution to the promotion of the sport and spirit of Judo.

Yours in Judo,

Robin Otani

Robin Otani (5th Dan).

INTRODUCTION

The martial art of Judo has been structured as a combative sport, making it possible for individuals to employ their fighting skills, one against the other, in either free-practice or contest situations.

Unlike some other martial art forms, Judo as a sport is confined by rules to the use of throws, hold-downs, strangles and arm-locks. All can be freely and fully applied by the Tori (attacker) upon the Uke (defender), who learns to nullify or counter them by correct break-falling, escapes or, as a last resort, timely and safe submission. Other locks, as well as kicks or blows with the hand, arm or fist, are not allowed in the interest of safety from injury.

However, many of the more injurious and deadly techniques that are applied with foot and fist, so flamboyantly portrayed in Karate and Kung Fu martial arts films, can be learned by the judoka (Judo player) who chooses to study the Judo katas (referred to on page 135) under the guidance of a senior instructor. Perhaps in today's violent climate, Judo may have sold itself short (not that it needs to sell anything) in preferring to lay the emphasis of its art upon the manner in which it can be performed and enjoyed as a sport. But, make no mistake about it, an experienced judoka who is proficient in all aspects of his chosen martial art is a formidable and spectacular opponent for anyone.

Judo is practised (or studied) by men and women, boys and girls; sometimes even whole families become involved in the sport. To whatever association or governing body any particular Judo club belongs, there is generally a training syllabus and progressive grading examinations set down for males and females at both junior and senior levels. This enables the successful student to progress upwards through the Kyu (student) grades of white, yellow, orange, green, blue and brown belts up to the coveted black belt of a 1st Dan and beyond.

Provided that any aspiring Judo player is reasonably fit and healthy, there is little to prevent him or her from taking up the sport. Naturally, it is advisable for a beginner taking up a strenuous pastimes of any sort to get a clean bill of health from their doctor beforehand. This applies particularly to people who have not been active in a sport of any kind for some time, and who are perhaps not quite so young as they once were.

Age in itself, however, presents no barrier to the healthy person wishing to play Judo. Many beginners come into the sport when they are already in their vintage years as far as competitive sport is concerned. Such judoka may not be potential gold medallists, but many prove capable of working diligently through their syllabus to emerge eventually as high Kyu or even Dan grades. Whatever they achieve, they bring a welcome element of maturity into the clubs. They become capable of providing hard practice sessions for up-and-coming youngsters and are eligible to serve the sport in general as administrators, instructors, referees and officials of one sort or another.

For all these reasons, a Judo career can be long and enjoyable, particularly for those who remain fit enough to continue with even a small amount of randori after their contest days are over. Such mat veterans often prove that their mature patience and skill can overcome the exuberance of younger players — running out of good old-fashioned breath is usually the main handicap of the older player.

On the subject of handicaps, I have known blind students who have progressed reasonably well through the Kyu grades to prove themselves worthy opponents, especially when grappling on the ground, where stability and balance are not so crucial. Deaf players, too, do as well as anyone else, provided that those responsible for the mat upon which they appear are always first made aware of their handicap. Both judoka and officials must recognize the need for the deaf player's immediate response to firm body slaps, which have to replace vocal commands to freeze or stop and withdraw from any action.

At what age can youngsters take up Judo? Junior players are usually accepted into clubs from the age of six years upwards. They become Seniors around the age of sixteen. Players usually peak around their mid-twenties and might then retain that standard of performance for the next ten years. Between about thirty-five and forty-five years of age players acquire technical maturity. After that age, a natural decline in speed, suppleness and stamina follows, but not necessarily of pure skill. With continued practice, the latter should always remain.

Such, then, are the sort of people who pract-

Brian Caffary (4th Dan) pictured on the mat.

INTRODUCTION

ise Judo and who are always welcome to the ranks of our beginners from all walks of life. It is probably true to say that in no other fiercely competitive sport do those who are already experienced or accomplished display such endless patience and perseverance in helping and teaching those of lower grades. Perhaps it is because the longer you are in Judo, the more you realize just how much can still be learned — and not only from grades senior to your own. A sensei (teacher) may have no prouder or more fulfilling moment than when a student reaches or even surpasses his (or her) own level of qualification.

Nevertheless, students themselves must also display determination and discipline in order to bring this about. Not everyone taking up Judo is, or needs to be, contest-minded. Provided that a judoka takes the sport itself seriously, he or she will be coached and encouraged with equal enthusiasm whether they want to compete or do no more than make progress through the gradings. What a student cannot do is to take Judo too casually. It's not a sport which you can turn to only spasmodically because you feel that there's no real teamwork involved and therefore you won't be letting anyone down by your absence. You will: you'll be letting yourself down. Progress in Judo is slow and hard. To slip back is quick and easy, and then no one derives any benefit from your unfit, unskilled appearances on the mat.

Assuming that you have decided to take up the sport of Judo, the first thing is to enquire about tutorial and training facilities in your area. There is nothing wrong with evening classes run by local authorities if you want a 'sampler' before going in for the real thing. However, if you wish to savour the real atmosphere of the sport, to experience competitive bite, and to be able to meet and talk Judo with other judoka at all levels as well as benefiting from their varied experience, there is no substitute for a club.

This book explains all the the techniques needed to progress through all the grades from beginner to blackbelt. Whilst there may be differences of technique and particular syllabus requirements between different clubs and associations, what is common is the Japanese language of Judo which, like it or not, must be learned. One benefit of this is that you can walk into any Judo club anywhere in the world and communicate successfully, for the sport's language is universal.

Individual techniques are also common, but there always have been and always will be slight differences in the exact manner in which their application is taught regardless of the teacher's governing body. So, please don't argue too much with your club's sensei — or with this book if someone else's method of applying a particular technique differs from mine.

I have attempted in this book to present each technique as I would to students in a class. Photographs demonstrate the key movements in a technique, each with a descriptive caption. Some general information is given about the technique itself and then special coaching points to which you should pay particular attention.

No book can ever replace personal tuition from a sensei in the dojo (practice hall), though it is my hope that the effort that has gone into the preparation of this volume will provide both an armchair manual of revision for students and a matside reference for those working on the development of particular techniques.

A word of warning to beginners — never attempt the dangerous practice of trying things out on your own with a partner but minus a mat and a qualified instructor. It may be all right later on when you are experienced perhaps, but it should certainly not be tried to begin with.

Finally, I wish you all a long and enjoyable career in Judo. Work hard and the rewards will come.

THE HISTORY OF JUDO

Despite the development of so many types of weaponry, unarmed combat has remained a skill to be practised by civilians and soldiers alike all over the world. Different styles of unarmed fighting gradually evolved throughout history. While some were similar to others, each placed its own emphasis upon particular powers and techniques, so that eventually many became recognized as specific and individual martial art forms.

Almost all martial art forms surviving today have roots buried deep in oriental history, the exact origin of many lost in the mists of time. Some historians have even questioned whether Jujitsu, from which Judo was evolved, actually originated in Japan, though there appears little doubt that this was the country in which Jujitsu became really developed and perfected as a distinctive form of martial art. Sometimes referred to as Jujutsu (or Taijutsu, or Yawara), Jujitsu was used commonly by warriors in battle during Japan's great feudal age. Legend recounts the chivalry of Japan's great knights being such that they would never take unfair advantage of an opponent, so if an adversary became disarmed or deprived of his weapons in battle, the gallant Japanese knight discarded his own to engage the enemy in unarmed combat.

Many such knights soon found themselves in need of special training in the application of what must have been initially a series of random blows, kicks and wild attempts at choking or throwing an opponent to the ground. Special training centres were established at which knights were taught by experts all the sophistication of what was coming to be known as Jujitsu.

By the late sixteenth century, Jujitsu was being taught in Japan in a structured and methodical manner. For the next 250 years or so, it continued developing into an increasingly complicated art of attack and defence, and was taught by masters of many different schools.

Among latter-day students of that era was a young man named Jigoro Kano. Born in 1860, he studied Jujitsu under several great teachers of the day while pursuing his academic career at Tokyo Imperial University. The young Kano was forever perplexed by the differing teaching principles of each Jujitsu teacher. It seemed to him that, while each taught a range of techniques, none had grasped the total concept of all Jujitsu, discovered its true essence or what lay behind it all. Searching diligently for a simple underlying principle which was applicable to all techniques, he was eventually able to define the common principle as being the need to maximize the total efficiency of both mental and physical energy in the application of all techniques.

With this somewhat broad theory in mind, Kano carefully analysed all Jujitsu methods of both attack and defence. All techniques which he considered to fall short of his principle he either rejected or substituted with his own change or modification. These, along with Jujitsu techniques of which he did approve, became grouped together into a new martial art which he called Judo.

In Jujitsu and Judo, the first part of each word, 'ju', means 'gentleness' or 'giving way'. In Jujitsu, 'jitsu' means 'art' or 'practice'; in Judo, 'do' means 'principle' or 'way'. Whereas Jujitsu may be loosely translated to mean 'the gentle art', Kano's new martial art of Judo was 'the way of gentleness,' or 'the gentle way'.

The structure of Judo as a martial art was categorized or graded by Kano in such a way that it could be practised as a competitive sport with reasonable safety from unnecessary injury. Blows, kicks, certain types of joint locks, and other techniques considered too dangerous for use in open competition, were removed from the general syllabus but retained for teaching to higher grades and others qualified to study certain forms of Judo kata.

Young Kano's devotion to the formulation and establishment of Judo did not interfere with his academic progress. He pursued his study of literature, politics and political economy and graduated from Tokyo Imperial University in 1881. One year later, at the age of only twenty-three Professor Kano (as he became known) founded the Kodokan School for Judo; a memorial stone commemorating the occasion rests in the Buddhist Temple Eishoji.

The Kodokan's headquarters is now a splendid modern building, the Kodakan International Judo Centre, situated in the Bunkyo Ward of Tokyo. These multi-storied premises provide several dojos, changing and rest rooms, lodging accommodation, conference and exhibition facilities, administrative offices and a Judo Hall of Fame. All this, and the spread of Judo's popularity throughout the world, remains a tribute to the pioneering work of Professor Kano.

Apart from his beloved Judo, Professor Kano

THE HISTORY OF JUDO

went on to enjoy an academic career as an educationalist of some distinction. He was a member of his country's Imperial House Department. In 1909 he became the first representative of his country to sit on the International Olympic Committee. Two years later the Japanese Amateur Sports Association was founded and he became its first president. Finally, a lifetime devoted to education and sport, and to Judo in particular, was sadly ended when Professor Kano died on board ship while returning home from an IOC meeting in Cairo in 1938.

Apart from having been such a great innovator and administrator, Professor Kano was a skilled performer on the mat. One famous story tells of a high-ranking judoka who, when asked about his experience of having competed against Kano, is reported to have said, 'It was like fighting with an empty jacket!'

Certainly in Professor Kano's early days, relatively few outside of Japan knew much about the art of Judo, let alone practised the sport. Perhaps Britain's first introduction to what it all meant was in 1892 when Takashima Shidachi lectured the Japan Society in London about the history and development of Judo. There followed several comings and goings of Japanese masters to Britain, but they were concerned more with the doctrines of Jujitsu than Judo. Then, in 1906, Gunji Koizumi arrived in Liverpool to teach Jujitsu. He went on to the United States of America the following year, but returned to Britain in 1910. Eight years later he opened Europe's first amateur Judo club in London's Grosvenor Place, the still-famous Budokwai, though its premises have since changed. The Budokwai's first senior instructor was Yukio Tani.

The year 1920 was a memorable one for British Judo because the esteemed Professor Kano himself visited our shores, accompanied by Hikoichi Aida (4th Dan) who was appointed Kodokan Coach to the Budokwai. Meanwhile, in 1919, a young man who was later to become the President of the British Judo Council, Masutaro Otani, had arrived in England. He continued with his study of the martial arts, particularly Judo, under Hikoichi Aida and became assistant instructor to Yukio Tani in 1926.

Apart from activity among a relatively small number of devotees, there were perhaps no really momentous happenings so far as Judo in Britain was concerned in the years that followed. Then, during the Second World War,

people of all nations found themselves plunged into military service. They were put through fitness routines and received varying degrees of training in what were Judo-based unarmed combat skills. Those selected for commando and special services training often achieved a high standard of expertise.

All these and other factors contributed towards the emergence of a post-war interest in Judo, not only in Britain but throughout the world. Masutaro Otani founded the Jubilee Judo Club in London during 1945. The British Judo Association was founded in 1948 and the European Judo Union came into being during the same year. Otani founded the Masutaro Otani School of Judo in 1954 and K. Abbe started the British Judo Council in 1958. Meanwhile, the Amateur Judo Association had been formed in 1956. By the time the MOSJ and the British Judo Council became amalgamated in 1970, the sport was establishing a strong presence in Britain and elsewhere at all levels of participation.

Japan was host nation to the 1964 Olympics, and Judo was given its first opportunity as a Games event in Tokyo. Some indication of the global spread of the sport by that time is perhaps reflected in the records of those Olympic Games. Of the sixteen medal awards, Japanese competitors won only three of the four gold medals, and only one of the four silvers. Of the remainder, the famous Dutch heavyweight Geesink took the open-category gold, and other medals were shared by competitors from the USSR, West Germany, South Korea, Austria and the United States.

Judo was dropped from the Mexico Games of 1968, but was reinstated for Munich in 1972. It has remained an Olympic event ever since, though confined to male competitors only up to and including the 1984 Games.

Dave Starbrook brought back Britain's first Olympic medal for Judo when he carried off the silver at Munich in 1972 in the 93-kg-and-under category. Britain enjoyed a double success at Montreal in 1976 with great performances from heavyweight Keith Remfry and, again, Dave Starbrook. Still suffering from the effects of a terrible chest injury sustained in his previous contest, Remfry bravely went on to the mat to fight Japan's Uemura for gold in the open category. The contest finished quickly, Remfry having to be content with the silver medal. On that occasion, Starbrook (still in the under-93s) brought back a bronze medal.

Four years later, Britain's much-fancied Brian Jacks had to settle for bronze in the under-86s, but of course went on to become a TV personality and almost a household name. Later, Neil Adams scored both Olympic and World Championship success.

The year 1980 saw Britain's first ever World Champion when Jane Bridge brought home the gold. However, Karen Briggs then became probably Britain's greatest international competitor to date, winning three consecutive World Championship titles (in the 48-kg-and-under category) in 1982, 1984 and 1986. With such strengths emerging from Britain's female ranks, great things may happen when Olympic Judo is opened up to include women competitors.

Masutaro Otani (8th Dan), late president of the British Judo Council.

PREPARING FOR JUDO

In comparison with many other sports and pastimes, Judo requires only a relatively low-budget investment on the part of the beginner. Basic requirements are a judogi (suit), club or evening class enrolment and, through that, registration with one of the organizing authorities for the sport.

If insurance is not automatically available through your club membership or national body association, it is advisable to ensure that you are insured against personal injury. This should not be taken as alarming advice, but should

Tying the belt

1 Hold the belt at its centre point in front of your waist.

2 Pass the ends around your back and forward again to the front, ensuring that both ends are of equal length.

be regarded in the same way as insuring your house: it is simply common sense. Thankfully, though, very much as a result of the safety-consciousness of all concerned with the organization and practice of the sport, serious injury in Judo is not a frequent occurrence.

On the subject of medical matters, it is advisable to have a check-up with your doctor before taking up Judo, especially if you have not undertaken any strenuous physical exercise for a long while.

Most instructors will allow beginners to practise for the first few weeks wearing only a tracksuit or any strong, loose clothing without buttons before investing in a judogi.

Judogi is the collective term for the jacket, trousers and belt. The trousers are held up by a tie-string drawn through the back of the waistband and bow-tied at the front. Both male and female players wear jackets in the same manner: first, push the right side of the jacket firmly across to the left hip, then draw the left side over the top towards the right hip. The mid-point of the belt is held against the centre abdomen at waist height and drawn twice around the body to be tied at the front in a flat reef knot with ends of equal length.

Female players wear a standard white T-shirt beneath the

3 Pass one end under both bands of the belt and pull tight.

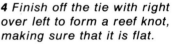

4 Finish off the tie with right over left to form a reef knot, making sure that it is flat.

jacket. Males are also sometimes allowed for either health or climatic conditions to do this, with the special permission of their sensei. Similar permission must be sought by both sexes for the wearing of socks on the mat, which also might be necessary for reasons of health or climate.

Most players wear ordinary trainers or slip-on shoes when away from the mat area itself, while others invest in the traditional flat sandal. Whatever footwear you choose, you must be able to slip it off easily; this is best performed by standing with your back to the mat, heels almost touching its edge, so that you step backwards out your shoes, one foot at a time, directly onto the mat. Coming off the mat, you simply step straight into your shoes again.

ETIQUETTE & DISCIPLINE

The term dojo (practice hall) is reputedly derived from an old Buddhist phrase meaning 'hall of enlightenment'. It is a place in which Judo is taught and practised and in which contests, training sessions and demonstrations (kata) take place. Wherever it is situated, however modestly or richly it is equipped, it is the place around which your Judo life will revolve throughout your connection with the sport.

A club dojo can be sited in any type of premises. Some are in a modest church hall, others in a modern sports complex. The location is immaterial so long as the area is large enough to accommodate the required numbers of members, and they can practise and break-fall in safety.

Every Judo dojo has its tatami (mat) spread over the floor to absorb the impact of falling bodies. The dojo is swept clean and should have an atmosphere of respect in order to stimulate the dedication and discipline demanded of the players.

Initially this respect is shown by all judoka performing ritsu-rei (standing bow) towards the dojo when entering or leaving it or towards the sensei when stepping on to or off the mat.

At no time must a judoka (or anyone else) walk upon the mat unless his or her feet are bare. Health and climatic reasons for waiving this rule have already been referred to and, of course, officials are permitted to wear socks at competitions and gradings.

Once upon the mat, a judoka is expected to peform ritsu-rei when requesting the sensei's permission to leave or come back on to it, and before and after addressing the sensei for any other reason. Similarly, partners perform ritsu-rei to each other before and after a practice or working together or during the performance of kata (demonstration). These rules apply unless, of course, players are involved in ground-

Standing bow ritsu-rei

1 *Stand relaxed, feet together, arms by your sides with hands on thighs.*

2 *From this posture perform ritsu-rei (standing bow) by dipping the top of your body slightly forward from the waist without removing your eyes from the subject of salutation, and then return immediately to a normal upright posture. Don't dip too deeply and don't look down at the mat.*

work, in which case they perform za-rei (kneeling bow).

It is customary and respectful, apart from reasons of basic hygiene, for all judoka to present themselves on the mat wearing a clean judogi, to be bodily clean and to have both fingernails and toenails neatly trimmed short. Long or jagged nails can be the cause of self-injury as well as harming an opponent.

For similar reasons of safety, players must remove all types of jewelry before stepping on to the mat — rings, necklaces, bracelets, wrist watches, hair clips and slides, and any other type of adornment that could scratch or tear skin or be the cause of any sort

of injury. Long hair, on male or female, is usually tied back and held in place by any sort of elasticated grip.

Satisfied that you are properly presented, your sensei will then direct you through the bowing-on ceremony which precedes any gathering on the mat. (It is repeated at the end of the gathering when it is referred to as bowing-off.) This brief ceremonial is an exchange of respect between the sensei and his students. Students (Kyu grades) are ranged in order of grade seniority from their left, beginning with the highest, as they face the sensei (and any other Dan grade or guest) on the opposite side of the mat. The side of the

Kneeling bow za-rei

1 The sensei kneels opposite his students to exchange za-rei (kneeling bow).

2 They all lean forward to place their left hand flat on the mat just to the right of the left knee, fingers pointing inwards.

3 The right hand is similarly placed to the left of the right knee as the students simultaneously bend forward to full za-rei. The sensei's feet are correctly placed, one overlapping the other.

4 All return to the upright position.

ETIQUETTE & DISCIPLINE

dojo on which the students stand along the mat is called shimoza and the side upon which the sensei and others appear is called kamiza.

On the sensei's command, 'sei-za', both he and his students will kneel. On a command from the senior Kyu grade on the extreme left of the line as it faces the sensei, all the students will perform za-rei (kneeling bow) towards the sensei who simultaneously reciprocates.

From then on, students must continue to show respect for the sensei by responding to his tutoring and discipline. It goes without saying that fooling around on a Judo mat is dangerous and is not allowed. Practise only that which you have been taught. Maintain as much silence as possible. Silence is not only an aid to concentration, but it also enables everyone to hear and react instantly to the sensei's commands and instructions.

Concerning the latter, it is important to learn two Japanese words you will hear often and which you must understand — hajime (begin) and matte (stop). To either command students must show immediate response regardless of what or where they are practising on the mat.

When it comes to practice, any judoka should regard it as an honour to be invited to work with a player of higher grade. Higher grades are almost without exception well versed in the etiquette of teaching lower grades without taking advantage of their comparative inexperience.

All the above points provide a basis for good Judo etiquette and self-discipline in the dojo.

Kneeling sei-za

1 Sensei Caffary demonstrates sei-za (kneeling), dropping first on to his left knee, his left hand by his left side and his right hand on his right knee.

2 Next, the right knee is dropped and the right hand drops to the right side.

3 Finally, he sits back on the heels of his crossed feet, hands on top of his thighs. Note how the top part of his body remains upright throughout the movement. The whole movement will be performed in exact reverse order when rising.

BALANCE & MOVEMENT

Whenever a judoka stands upon the mat, a straight leg (or legs) is not recommended. A supporting straight leg locks the joints and can in itself prove tiring. Being caught on a straight leg by an opponent in either practice or contest can not only be defeating but injurious too.

Shizentai (natural posture) is the basic posture in Judo, and there are three positions. In shizen-hontai the judoka stands relaxed with arms hanging loose. The legs are

Posture

1 *A judoka stands in shizentai (natural posture).*

not rigidly straight, but neither are they fully bent. Body weight is spread equally over both feet, which should be positioned apart somewhere in line with your own shoulder width. Toes point slightly outwards.

In migi-shizentai, the right foot only is placed slightly forward of the left foot. In hidari-shizentai, the left foot only is placed slightly forward.

There are also three forms of jigotai, the basic defence posture, which can also be used so effectively in attack when performing, say, kata-guruma (see page 36). The main and obvious changes in

posture from shizentai are the widening of the feet and the increased bending of the knees to drop the hips and thereby lower the body's centre of gravity. The feet, with

Taking hold

2 *Both players in natural right-side posture take hold of each other in the standard fashion — left hand gripping the underside of the opponent's right sleeve while the right hand grasps the left lapel with the thumb inside at a point about midway between shoulder and waist.*

toes pointed slightly out-wards, are clamped firmly on to the mat to share the body weight and form a sound and solid base.

In migi-jigotai you merely take one short step forward with the right leg only. In hid-ari-jigotai you take one step forward with the left leg only.

Almost all the throwing tech-niques demonstrated in this book are referred to as being executed from 'a natural right-side posture'. It is from this natural right-side (or right-handed) posture that you first take up the normal grip on your partner or opponent in the basic and traditional manner. Grasp the underside of his right forearm sleeve with your

left hand. Slide the thumb of your right hand inside the left lapel of his jacket at about mid-chest height and grip with a clenched fist, fingers on the outside. When tightening this grip on the lapel, do not forget to use your little and ring fin-gers to maximize the strength of your hold.

As you progress, not only through this book, but also later in any competitive career you may embark upon, you will find many variations within the rules on this basic manner of grasping your opponent's jacket. Sometimes it may be a sleeve and the back of his collar you will get hold of, his sleeve and the back of his jacket or even his belt, both

lapels or perhaps both sleeves. These changes are determined by the type of throw being executed, the need for some counter-action to an opponent's movement or (in many cases) the evolution of any individual's particular style of Judo.

Remember that you may only hold on to your op-ponent's belt in the course of executing a technique and that you must never hold any part or parts of one side only of his jacket for longer than three or four seconds. Also, you must not grab the inside of an opponent's sleeve or screw it up at the end. Nor are you per-mitted to hold on to the inside of your opponent's trouser leg

Breaking balance (kusushi)

1 Tori (on the left) senses instantly that he can break balance to Uke's rear right corner.

2 Tori sweeps with his left foot.

3 Tori throws Uke with ko-soto-gari (minor outer reaping).

either when standing or when engaged in groundwork.

Your gripping hands should be held firm but not clenched hard until the instant you attempt to break your opponent's balance in order to apply a technique.

When you and your partner have learned to get hold of each other correctly in the basic manner, you must next master walking each other forwards, backwards and sideways in every direction. An advancing and retreating movement is called shintai; a turning movement is called tai-sabaki.

In shintai (moving forwards, sideways and backwards) you should walk from the hips,

retaining the distribution of your body weight equally over both feet. Then slide rather than take deliberate steps with your feet.

As you begin to experience movement over the mat with a partner, so can you begin to feel or sense points at which he will be vulnerable and in a position for you to execute kusushi (to break the balance): that is, a position in which he will have tipped his body weight too far over a supporting leg and be exposed to a pull or push off balance in one direction or another.

Generally throughout this book Tori (the attacker) is referred to as breaking the balance of the Uke (the defen-

der) to the front or rear, to left side or right side. Additionally, there are right and left front corners and right and left rear corners to which balance can be broken.

A partner's balance forward is broken basically by pulling him up and forwards on to his toes and simultaneously tipping him to left or right by pushing and pulling on his jacket lapel and sleeve in the required direction. When doing this, your arms should be bent and rotate in a steering-wheel action. The same steering-wheel action is used to break balance to the rear, but in such cases, of course, your partner is first pushed back on to his heel or heels.

UKEMI

Many beginners take up Judo having thought of it only in terms of themselves performing the throws rather than being thrown, but for every judoka throwing, another must obviously fall. How to fall safely and to avoid — or at least minimize — any shock or injury on contact with the mat, therefore, are very much a part of the art of Judo and must rank highly among first things to be learned by a newcomer.

Ukemi is the term used to describe a series of break-fall techniques which reduce the impact of a fall if properly executed; this enables the player being thrown to land on the mat in comparative safety. Ma-ukemi is the art of falling forwards with safety, yoko-ukemi is falling sideways and ushiro-ukemi is falling backwards.

The basic principle of ukemi, practised by the player being thrown, is that the body should be relaxed and curled up as it passes through the air. Initial impact with the mat is absorbed by an arm (or both arms) being flung out to strike the mat on the side the fall is being made. The hand of the outstretched arm is held flat, palm facing downwards, and the arm itself is uncoiled swiftly from the shoulder to strike the mat flat as the landing is being made. An arm flung out flatly from shoulder to fingertips prevents those injuries to arms or shoulders which can occur if a landing is made on the points of the elbows.

During the fall, the judoka keeps the chin tucked down on to the chest so that the back of the head is not whiplashed back on to the mat. The leg on the side towards which the fall

Sideways rolling break-fall (yoko-kaiteri-ukemi)

1 Intending to fall across his left shoulder, the judoka raises his left arm and looks towards his left side as his left leg begins to bend.

2 He bends forward over his bent left knee as his left arm descends in a scooping movement towards a spot between his feet. There is already a smooth curve developing from his left fingertips, up the arm and across his back to the right shoulder.

3 The judoka has collapsed his left knee and allowed himself to roll down on to the mat right round that curve, throwing his right arm straight out behind him.

is made is relaxed and more or less in line with the body. The knee of the other leg is raised up slightly across the groin — many believe this protects the lower abdomen against further attack. In a sideways break-fall, the outstretched arm should strike the mat in position best described as a four o'clock on the right and eight o'clock on the left as the player is lying face upwards.

Good break-falls don't necessarily have to be seen to be appreciated — they can be heard loud and clear as those outstretched shock-absorbing arms smack on to the mat. It is not unnatural for beginners to have an inherent fear or at least some degree of nervousness about committing themselves freely to falling, but it is amazing how quickly they abandon themselves to the

Sideways break-fall (yoko-ukemi)

1 Intending to throw himself into the air and fall to his right side, the judoka stands with feet apart, right arm raised sideways and left knee preparing to take his weight.

2 The judoka looks towards the spot on which he will land and his right arm simultaneously swings down as his right leg begins a big swing upwards and across the front of his left leg.

3 With the momentum of his swinging arm and sweeping

leg action, the judoka throws himself into the air, that right arm already uncurling as it travels down again to his the mat and break the fall.

4 The right arm extends flat to break the fall and absorb the full initial impact of the body landing on the mat.

experience after careful tuition has taken them through progressive stages.

As a student you might begin by first lying flat on your back with your arms crossed well over your chest to touch each opposite shoulder. Then fling each arm out sideways alternately to strike the mat alongside in the manner described above; you may roll slightly from side to side as you perform this action. Next you may sit up and fall sideways with a break-fall action, or backwards to break-fall with both arms simultaneously.

As you become more adventurous, you can attempt rolling sideways and backwards from a squatting posture and throwing out an arm (or arms) to break the falls. From there, try sideways rolling break-falls from a feet-astride posture, bending forwards and rolling over one shoulder or the other. Sideways and backward break-falls may next be performed from a standing posture and then while on the move. Finally, you will be put to work with a partner and begin to experience break-falling to safe landings after actually being thrown.

Junior players are additionally taught to perform forward-rolling break-falls. These eventually become safe landings after what is more like a somersault through the air, without the hands touching the mat until the point of impact on landing. Some sensei also teach a forward-falling break-fall in which the player lands on flat raised forearms, with feet astride on turned-in toes to raise the hips off the mat, and head turned sideways to avoid facial injury.

Backward break-fall (ushiro-ukemi)

1 *Intending to fall to his rear, the judoka stands with both arms raised in parallel in front of him.*

2 *Keeping his body upright, the judoka sinks to a crouch in readiness to jump in the air and throw himself to the rear.*

3 *As the judoka jumps to clear his feet from the mat and throw his legs up into the air, his body tips backwards to fall upon the mat — but not before those flat arms have made a resounding break-fall on each side of his body and absorbed most of the impact. Note also how his chin has been well tucked in and head held forward to prevent any whiplash effect on to the mat.*

WARMING UP

Whatever their seniority, all experienced players will almost habitually go through variable stretching routines and practise breakfalls in a warming-up process before starting their real work on the mat. How much time an instructor devotes to exercises and body-building routines in a class must depend upon how often the classes are held and how long each lasts.

Generally, however, in order to maintain a supple body and to build up strength and stamina, it's the responsibility of the judoka to exercise outside the time spent on the mat. Then, at the beginning of a Judo session, the sensei need concern himself only with leading his pupils through a warming up programme designed to loosen limbs from head to toe and generally stir up the circulation in readiness for a vigorous Judo work-out.

The warming-up exercise routine might well begin with jumping exercises followed by head-rolling, arm swings to rotate the shoulders, and trunk turning and twisting to loosen up the back. There should also be hip rolling with feet astride, and knee rolls performed with feet together. Ankle pulls should be performed in a sitting position with the feet wide apart, and there should also be press-ups, sit-ups, cat stretches and squat thrusts. Other important exercises include revolving the feet forwards and backwards from the ankle, and repeatedly rotating the hands inwards and outwards while holding them at arm's length. From there, it's into break-falls.

Hips, shoulders, legs, neck . . . all joints from head to toe are warmed up in a series of exercises before this group gets down to more serious work on the mat.

TECHNIQUES & PRACTICE

Exactly how your Judo education will begin on the mat depends very much upon your individual sensei, but it is likely to be in relation to a set syllabus which may vary slightly according to the policy of your club or parent organization. Over a period of time, any full syllabus should take a judoka through the range of two main categories of techniques as well as the necessary knowledge of kata (demonstrations, page 135). The two main categories are nage-waza (throwing techniques) and katame-waza (grappling on the mat, generally referred to as groundwork).

A third category of Judo techniques, atemi-waza, is concerned with the delivery of blows and kicks which are capable of causing dangerous or even fatal injury. For that reason they are practised only in kata and never in free practice or contest situations. Because a knowledge of them is not necessary in order to progress from beginner to black belt in Judo, they are not explained in this book.

The two main categories of techniques, nage-waza and katame-waza, are themselves each divided into further groups.

Nage-waza (throwing techniques) is subdivided into tachi-waza (standing techniques) and sutemi-waza (sacrifice techniques).

Tachi-waza is further divided into te-waza (hand techniques), koshi-waza (hip techniques) and ashi-waza (foot techniques).

Sutemi-waza are throws in which Tori (the attacker) must also fall on to the mat himself in the course of throwing an opponent. Sutemi-waza is divided into two groups of sacrifice techniques — ma-sutemi-waza, in which Tori must throw himself backwards in the course of executing the technique; and yoko-sutemi-waza, in which Tori throws himself sideways.

Katame-waza (groundwork techniques) is subdivided into osae-komi-waza (hold-down techniques), shime-waza (strangling or choking techniques) and kansetsu-waza (joint techniques). Although kansetsu-waza and shime-waza are grouped under the general category of groundwork techniques, always remember that strangles, chokes and arm-locks can often be applied also from a standing posture.

It is from this whole range of techniques that a syllabus might begin with throws such as o-soto-gari (major outer reaping) or ippon-seoi-nage (one-arm shoulder throw), and with groundwork such as kesa-gatame (scarf hold). Note that only arm-locks are allowed in competitive Judo. Leg-, wrist- and neck-locks, or any other type of technique which attacks joints, are not permitted. Neither is the grabbing or twisting of an opponent's fingers or thumbs.

Whatever techniques are embarked upon to begin with, the sensei will no doubt demonstrate them before pairing you off with a partner to try it for yourself under his supervision. Later, if he becomes satisfied also with your break-fall ability and general respect for dojo discipline and etiquette, he may release you for randori (free practice). In randori any number of pairs can be in practice combat on the mat at the same time. Each pair practises at its own pace and, unless directed otherwise by the sensei, works on whichever techniques it particularly wishes to develop.

The sensei may direct everyone to practise, say, o-uchi-komi, in which players take it in turn to perform perhaps nine turn-ins only on their partner and execute the full throw on the tenth. When performing o-uchi-komi, Tori takes the technique no further than performing the footwork for a particular throw as he moves in on his partner, pulling him to the point of break-balance, making full body contact and then stepping out again. Practice at this enables a judoka to perform o-uchi-komi confidently, smoothly and at speed comparable to that of a contest. It combines technical improvement with good exercise routine.

Finally, before moving on to the real techniques of Judo, remember that however hard the sensei works, any practice on the mat can only really be as hard and worthwhile as you want to make it for yourself — so work hard!

NAGE-WAZA
THROWING TECHNIQUES

For nage-waza, your arms should be neither straight nor held stiffly. Your grip on an opponent should be firm but relaxed as though holding reins and ready to pull or push instantly in whichever direction he is already moving. In that way you will use his energy and momentum to your own advantage as your propel him into a throw. The whole art of nage-waza is in being able to feel the direction in which an opponent is already moving and then simply help him on his way by adding your own force to pull, push or lift him through a throwing technique.

To begin with, and even later, you require perseverance and a patient partner in order to be able to perform nage-waza with any sort of ease or effectiveness. Occasionally, though, you will manage 'a good one', and this will give you a tremendous feeling of achievement and encouragement to progress to the next technique.

Don't forget that if you are Uke in this practising partnership, you must commit yourself to being thrown. Resistance to a throw not only ruins the practice, but can also be the cause of injury. Relax, go with the throw and regard it all as valuable break-falling experience.

TE-WAZA

Properly executed, tai-o-toshi is a technique which enables a small man to throw a bigger opponent, because the main element required for success is timing. The size, strength or weight of your opponent is generally irrelevant if the timing of your tai-o-toshi is correct — that is, if you initially catch your opponent off balance at precisely the right moment. Then you must synchronize the timing of your hands, hips and legs in order to carry out the whole technique effectively.

It may sound as though a great deal of your body is at work to apply what is simply categorized as te-waza (hand techniques). However, tai-o-toshi is a popular contest technique for all the obvious reasons (economy of effort being one).

1 Attacking from a natural right-side posture, Tori pulls Uke forward on to his toes and at the same time pushes to the left with his right hand as it holds Uke's left lapel. Simultaneously, Tori pulls on Uke's right sleeve with his left hand. Already Tori has moved his left foot into position about opposite Uke's left foot and is about to pivot and swing his right foot tightly round behind it.

2 As Tori pivoted on his left foot, his right foot has swung into position outside Uke's right foot. Tori's hips are clear to the left of Uke whose body balance is being broken to his right front corner.

3 As Tori completes the turn to his own left, his head looks to the left where Uke will break-fall on to the mat. Pulling Uke on a circular route, Tori presses his toes into the mat to straighten the knee of his propping right leg and at this point Uke's legs flip into the air.

Use both hands to pull your opponent off balance. Keep your right elbow down when pulling him towards you. Then, as you begin to turn in, curl your right fist as for ippon-seoi-nage and drive the tip of your right elbow only (not the fore-arm) into your opponent's right armpit for extra leverage.

Keep your left elbow up as you pull your opponent in a circular movement towards his right front corner. Do not pull with a downward movement until you are completing the technique.

4 Without any full body contact having been made, Uke is spun through the air around Tori to break-fall in front of his attacker. Tori maintains a grip on Uke's right sleeve to remain in contact and in control in the event that the referee might award him something less than 'Ippon!' and he has to follow through with an arm-lock or some other groundwork technique.

Turn so that your hips are well clear to the left side of your opponent.

Straighten out your right leg with a vigorous jerk to maximize the 'flip' effect it will have as your opponent is jerked into the air.

TACHI-WAZA

Performed correctly, ippon-seoi-nage is considered to be a throw which typifies the art of Judo in as much as you maximize the forward momentum of your opponent's own weight and energy to enable you to throw him over your shoulder. To put it more simply, you haul him on to your back and toss him over your shoulder without much apparent effort.

Because it is much easier to throw an opponent whose centre of gravity is higher than your own, this is a technique which often proves effective against a taller and sometimes heavier opponent.

1 Tori takes hold of Uke's top outer right sleeve and pulls forward to break Uke's balance towards his right front corner. At the same time, Tori will step across to place his right foot opposite the inside of Uke's left foot. Note that Tori is already beginning to turn and move his own right arm towards Uke's outstretched right arm.

2 Bending his knees, Tori has now moved his right foot, swung his left foot round behind him and pivoted, so he finishes with both feet pointing forwards and in line with those of Uke. Tori's upper right arm is firmly lodged up into Uke's armpit, and Uke is pulled up on to his toes and begins to bend over Tori's back.

3 As Tori begins to straighten his legs, Uke is taken further off the mat. At the same time Tori pulls Uke's right arm hard across his own chest while driving his upper right arm into Uke's left armpit so that Uke is thrown forward over Tori's right shoulder.

Move in with bent knees and push your hind-quarters firmly into the lower abdomen of your opponent as you pull hard on his right arm to begin raising him off the mat and on to your back.

Keep your right upper arm lodged firmly in your opponent's armpit — don't let it slip down into the inside of his elbow or leverage will be lost and its lifting power completely ineffective.

4 As the throw is completed, note how Tori has now almost straightened his legs, retains his balance and keeps a firm hold of Uke's left sleeve.

Don't turn in so far that your left hip ends up in front of your opponent's right hip and he is bent diagonally across your back — you will never get him over your right shoulder! Ideally, you should turn in so that, on completion of the turn, both your feet are between those of your opponent and pointing forwards in the direction in which the throw is to be made.

TE-WAZA

In a morote-seoi-nage, just as in the ippon-seoi-nage, you utilize the forward-moving energy of an opponent to your own advantage in a manner which enables you to throw him over your shoulder with much greater ease. The major difference between the two techniques is in the use of your right arm. The major similarity between them is their effectiveness against taller opponents and the need to begin by turning in to your adversary with springy knees already in a bent posture — the lower the better.

Of the two techniques, morote-seoi-nage is the one you're less likely to find effective against a stiff-armed opponent as the need to keep hold of his left lapel with your right hand may make the initial turning-in a difficult movement.

1 Tori begins by pulling hard on Uke's right sleeve in order to raise Uke on to his toes before breaking his balance forward. His right hand (which is hidden from the camera) is gathering a curled-in fistful of the left lapel of Uke's jacket.

2 With the essential crouching legs, Tori has crossed over with his right foot, swung his left foot round behind him and pivoted, so that both his feet are in line and facing the direction of the throw. Tori has simultaneously punched his forearm up into Uke's right armpit and is also pulling on Uke's right arm so that, as Tori begins to bend, Uke is already raised up on to his toes and ready to be thrown.

3 Tori bends low and forward, his left arm kept close into his chest as Uke's right arm is pulled further around his body. At the same time, Tori's clenched right hand is punching through with a fistful of jacket to maximize the forearm lift, so that Uke's feet clear the mat and he is hauled over Tori's right shoulder.

At the outset take a good solid grip of your opponent's left lapel with your right hand, making a solid 'fist' which you curl inwards towards yourself and which stays that way throughout the execution of the technique.

4 As Tori completes the throw, pulling with his left hand and driving with his right, note how his head and the top half of his body face the direction in which Uke falls.

From this position of the curled-in 'fist' you will find it easier to pivot your bent arm upward so that your forearm fits solidly into a point of leverage beneath your opponent's right armpit.

For similar reasons of safety, keep your right wrist curled inwards. A common mistake is to allow your 'fist' to drag backwards against your own pulling power. If you allow this to happen, you will at least lose the technique's real punching power and at worst strain your wrist.

TE-WAZA

Morote-seoi-otoshi is like a combination of the arm movements of morote-seoi-nage (one-arm shoulder throw) with the leg movements of tai-otoshi (body drop).

1 In a natural right-side posture, Tori pulls on the underside of Uke's right sleeve to begin breaking balance to Uke's right front corner. Simultaneously Tori steps across to place his right foot on the outside of Uke's right foot. Tori's left foot is ready to be swung round behind him. Note that Tori is already beginning to slip his own right arm beneath Uke's outstretched right arm as for a seoi-nage.

2 With his left knee bent to take his weight, Tori extends his right leg as for tai-otoshi and it bends slightly as it rests against Uke's right front shin. Tori has slipped his right upper arm into Uke's right armpit for extra leverage and, as he turns to his left, he uses both hands to pull Uke's right arm around him. Uke's feet are already raised on tip-toe by Tori's lift-and-pull action.

Rather than turning right out from an opponent on whom you've failed to execute, say, an ippon seoi-nage, you can only half-turn and then whip back in to surprise him with morote-seoi-otoshi. The effect and counter-effect of these two rapid actions can catch your opponent unawares.

3 Tori turns his head towards the direction of the throw. He pulls hard on Uke's right sleeve, applies lift with his own bent right arm, bends well forward as he turns and finally snaps his right leg straight for the final effort of throwing Uke around him.

There is no real need to extend your right leg as far out as you might for a tai-otoshi just so long as it is positioned against your opponent's shin with the foot on the outside of his right foot. Make sure that your toes are turned under on the mat to provide maximum push at the moment of throw.

4 Uke has travelled around Tori, who retains hold of Uke to control his flight as well as to ensure that he turns to land flat on his back.

TE-WAZA

TACHI-WAZA

Kata-guruma can be associated with tomoe-nage (stomach throw) as it is one of Judo's more spectacular throws. It is one to which some beginners aspire too early and which they should not be encouraged to attempt until they have acquired the proper experience. Not only must Tori's legs be sufficiently strong and his sense of balance well developed in order to perform the technique, but Uke also must have become proficient in break-falling to ensure tumbling with safety from what could be a height of 1½ metres or more.

You will come across kata-guruma, along with ippon-seoi-nage and uki-otoshi in the first set of nage-no-kata (throwing forms).

1 Tori and Uke are facing each other in a natural right-side posture from which Tori will step forwards and downwards to place his right foot at a spot on the inside of Uke's right foot. Gripping with his left hand on the underside of Uke's right sleeve, he will carry Uke's right arm high and behind his own head, which will lower as he crouches. Tori's right hand will move from Uke's left lapel to the back of Uke's right thigh.

2 Tori has now lowered his hips and is in a squat posture. The right side of his face presses against the front of Uke's right thigh and his right arm is now firmly encircling that thigh to a point behind the knee.

3 Tori's left arm continues to pull Uke's body across the back of his shoulders. In one single movement Tori begins to stand up. He lifts Uke's legs clear of the mat on the right as his left arm continues to pull Uke's head and shoulders down his left side.

It is essential to wrap up your opponent's right thigh firmly by trapping it with your head, arm and shoulder. (OPPOSITE, BELOW) Don't have your feet too far apart when turned into the squat: too extreme a posture will make it more difficult to straighten your legs in order to lift your opponent clear of the mat.

When pulling with your left hand, (3, above) keep your left elbow close into your left side and bend in that direction also until your feel your opponent's weight leaving your shoulders.

In a randori (or contest) you might sometimes be slick enough to perform kata-guruma from almost a squat position without any real need to straighten up completely.

4 When Tori is almost upright he continues to pull hard down with his left hand and gives a push on Uke's legs with his right hand. This is when Uke finally tips over the point of balance across Tori's shoulders and break-falls lengthways in front of him.

TE-WAZA

Sumi-otoshi has similarities with uki-otoshi (floating drop). Both are hand techniques and there is no body contact between Tori and Uke in the course of their execution. Both are difficult to perform correctly and, though you will need to find an equally patient and persevering partner to perform them, you will eventually find that practice (and more practice!) will make perfect.

1 From a natural right-side posture Tori has stepped back to drop his hips and used his hands to draw Uke forward on to his right foot.

2 As Uke's right foot moves forward Tori turns his upper body to his left and swivels his left leg to stretch out along the outside of Tori's right leg. He pulls hard on Uke's right sleeve and pushes on his left lapel.

As your right leg bends to support your during this throw, you'll get extra power into your pull-through action by pushing off the toes of your right foot, while your curled right hand punches across into your opponent's left lapel.

3 By now, Tori's legs are spreadeagled and he is benefiting from Uke's own oncoming momentum. The turning of his own body, combined with the pull-and-push twisting action of his arms, will pull Uke off his feet and twirl him through the air towards Tori's left side.

To achieve the greatest effect from this hand throw, it is worth 'walking' your opponent about the mat for a while until his momentum is at a maximum as he comes towards you. It will then be his oncoming energy, as much as your own, that spins him off his feet and onto his back.

4 Tori retains his two-handed grip on Uke's jacket to make sure that he has flipped over to land upon his back.

TE-WAZA

A great deal of skill and timing is required in order to perform uki-otoshi properly and this technique is thus not normally found amongst general syllabus work. However, within the rules of the British Judo Council it is required that, outside syllabus work or contest success, a student must be able to demonstrate a knowledge of kata at certain stages of progress towards the achievement of black belt (1st Dan) status. Uki-otoshi is the first technique a student is called upon to demonstrate when performing nage-no-kata. Apart from that, it is a throw which epitomizes the spirit and principles of Judo by the manner in which an opponent's advancing movement and energy are converted into use against him.

1 Tori and Uke are each in a natural right-side posture Tori grips Uke's left lapel with his right hand and Uke's right inside upper sleeve with a reversed left-hand grip After pushing Uke backwards he will use Uke's resisting energy to reverse his movement and pull Uke towards him. Note how Tori is already beginning to transfer his own weight on to his right leg in readiness to drop on to his left knee.

2 Without any full body contact Tori has stepped back on the left foot and dropped to his left knee. At the same time his arms have pulled Uke around him into what is the beginning of a twirling motion.

3 Tori completes the action to pull Uke through the air with his hands. When demonstrating uki-otoshi in nage-no-kata, Tori would at this stage have placed his knee down on to the mat as demonstrated.

When asked to demonstrate uki-otoshi as part of nage-no-kata, you will be expected to perform the technique from a slow walk in partnership with your opponent. You will be the one taking two steps backwards, going down on one knee on the third step as you pull your opponent past you.

Making full use of your opponent's forward momentum, your right hand should pull strongly from right to left across his chest. It helps the turning power of your pull and gives you greater lift if at this stage of the throw you are able to push your right elbow up into your opponent's left armpit.

4 Tori has completed the throw and still retains control of Uke who has landed lengthways and slightly to the rear.

When pulling through to complete the full throw, begin to straighten your arms slightly so that your opponent falls clear of your left leg.

KOSHI-WAZA

A beginner may not at first find much apparent difference between uki-goshi and the more common o-goshi (major hip throw). The main difference is in the positioning of your hips into your opponent's abdomen. When executing uki-goshi, you do not turn in so far that both your hips are buried into his body. Neither do you bend your knees low or lean forward in order to raise your hips. Instead you employ a body twist which, combined with hand and arm action, tends to pull your opponent around your hip rather than over the top.

1 From a natural right-side posture Tori pulls on Uke's left arm to break his opponent's balance to his right front corner. Simultaneously, Tori's right foot will cross to a position opposite the inside of Uke's left foot in readiness to pivot. Tori's right arm is ready to slip around Uke's back.

2 Tori has pivoted on his right foot and turned left so that his right hip makes firm contact with Uke's abdomen. Tori's left foot is swinging round behind him, but not so far as for o-goshi. Tori pulls firmly on Uke's right sleeve, his elbow high in a circular route. Tori's right arm is slipped right around Uke's back to hug his opponent solidly to him.

3 Tori bends forward, though not so low as for o-goshi, completing the circular pull-and-push route of his arms so that Uke's feet leave the mat as his body begins to come around Tori's right hip.

As with o-goshi, you may prefer to grasp the back of your opponent's jacket if your require extra leverage to pull him in close for the lift.

To avoid your uki-goshi becoming o-goshi, remember not to bring your left foot too far round behind you on the turn in — it should end up in a position pointing roughly towards ten o'clock as you face forward after the turn.

4 Tori completes the throw with a quick twist of his hip combining with a final pull-through from his left arm so that Uke is thrown to the mat in front of him.

Work to develop a quick twist of the hip which, if co-ordinated with a strong arm action, should circulate your opponent around your hip and down upon the mat.

Harai-goshi is a hip technique which probably needs a little more practice to perfect than does o-goshi. The major differences between harai-goshi and o-goshi can be in the positioning of your right arm and hips when making contact with your opponent. In harai-goshi your right arm need not always wrap around the back of his body and your hips are not driven in quite so deeply as when executing o-goshi. The additional factor in harai-goshi, of course, is the employment of a leg sweep to help your opponent on his way.

Harai-goshi is particularly effective for use against a pushy opponent who constantly attempts to come in close and step around you as you attempt to throw him with other techniques.

1 From a natural right-side posture, Tori pulls on Uke's right sleeve to break his balance to the front right corner. Tori's right hand is curled around Uke's back and pushing towards Uke's right side. At the same time, Tori turns towards his own left and his right foot crosses to a position slightly further to left of centre between Uke's feet.

2 As Tori continues to turn he leans forward to drive his right hip into Uke's stomach below Uke's centre of gravity. Simultaneously, he has slid his left foot round behind him, transferred his weight on to it leaning forwards, and swept his straight right leg backwards and up against Uke's right leg.

3 As Tori's leg sweep reaches maximum height he gives a masterly jerk of his right hip to toss Uke into orbit and continues to pull Uke with his arms to land on the mat in front of him.

Don't let your sweeping leg develop a chopping action. Practise co-ordinating a twist of your hips with a long and smooth backward leg sweep in order to get the most effective results from this technique.

Become adept on both left and right sides and then practise the art of enticing an opponent in close enough to take him by surprise with this technique.

4 Tori gets both feet back on the mat in a balanced posture and holds firmly on to his opponent's left sleeve as Uke break-falls.

Against an opponent of equal size (or smaller), your sweeping leg should cross that of your opponent slightly above the knee. Against a taller opponent, the sweep should cross at just below knee height.

KOSHI-WAZA

As with most hip throws, the effectiveness of tsuri-komi-goshi depends very much upon your ability to make use of your opponent's forward momentum. As you turn in to him, his own advancing weight and energy are used to help propel him on to your hip and into the throw.

Sode-tsuri-komi-goshi (lift-pull sleeve hip throw) is a very similar throwing technique but you do not grasp your opponent's left lapel. Instead you take hold of the underside of his left sleeve with your right hand in a reverse grip with the clenched fingers pointing outwards. As you turn in, your opponent's left arm is first pushed straight up into the air and then across your right armpit, which is open as you lean forward to pull through and complete the throw.

1 From a natural right-side posture, Tori pulls hard on Uke's right sleeve with his left hand. He slides his right hand up Uke's left lapel to grasp his collar. From this position, Tori is able to pull Uke forward on to his toes. Meanwhile, Tori's right foot has moved across to a spot facing the inside of Uke's right foot and he has pivoted round upon it.

2 Tori has completed the pivot on his right foot. He has swung his left foot round behind him so that both his feet are now more or less in line with Uke's feet and pointing in the same direction. Tori's knees are bent in readiness for maximum lift as the hips drive into Uke's stomach.

3 Uke's feet leave the mat completely as Tori is at full bend forward and pulling Uke's right arm across his chest. Tori pushes through with his right forearm lodged beneath Uke's left armpit.

4 Tori straightens his legs and jerks his hip as he follows through with pull-and-push arm action to throw Uke so that he lands in front of him on the mat.

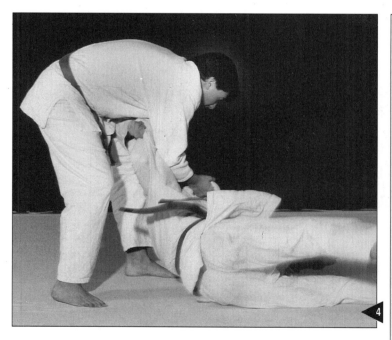

As with hip throws generally, you need to move in with knees already bending in readiness for legs to straighten in aid of a strong lift-off.

With tsuri-komi-goshi, the lower you can crouch as you turn in, the greater will be the leverage achieved with your arm action.

It is worth spending some time with a partner analysing and perfecting the full movement of your right arm in this technique. The tighter you can get your right forearm (not the point of your elbow) into your opponent's armpit, the more effective your lift will become.

The same need for right-arm action analysis, of course, also applies to those trying sode-tsuri-komi-goshi (see the general introduction to this technique). For this variant your opponent will also have to experience being thrown with both his arms initially tied up in your grip so that neither is free for a break-fall.

KOSHI-WAZA

TACHI-WAZA

Hane-goshi, as implied by its English translation 'hip spring' or 'spring hip', actually appears as a springy action when the technique is performed correctly. Your opponent then appears to be 'sprung off' your hip and into the air the instant you move in and make contact with his rising bent leg.

Often regarded as a good contest technique, the throw requires repeated practice to achieve real perfection. Probably more than in any other hip technique there is the need to develop the co-ordinated actions of your hands, hips and legs — especially the raised leg from which the springing action off your hip is activated.

Hane-goshi is also a good technique for incorporation into a sequence of combination techniques.

1 Tori and Uke are each in a natural right-side posture when Tori pulls on Uke's right sleeve and pushes his left lapel to break Uke's balance to the right front corner. Simultaneously, Tori will cross over with his advancing right foot, pivot round upon it and swing his left foot round behind him.

2 Tori transfers his weight on to that slightly bent left knee. Tori continues to turn and bend forward, pulling Uke tightly across the side of his body. Tori's right hip is driven solidly into Uke's stomach and his right knee is raised as his right instep is placed behind Uke's right calf.

3 Tori has continued to pull round to his left, pivoting on his left foot while straightening out his right leg. This action hoists Uke's legs high into the air. He is carried firmly up on to Tori's hip, at which point Tori jerks the hip and Uke 'springs' into the air.

Repeated practice will enable you to speed up the frozen-frame breakdown of movements shown on this page. Eventually you will appear to spring forward into action, turn, raise your leg and straighten it out and jerk your opponent off your hip and into the air, all in one fluid movement.

4 Tori's right leg comes down again to maintain solid balance as Uke break-falls in front of him.

Your raised bent knee should project to the front of your opponent's leg as you lean forward so that the whole side of your body, from your thigh through your hips to your chest, is making solid contact with the front of his body in readiness for that hip jerk.

Don't forget to straighten your supporting left leg at the final moment of making the throw to provide Uke with greater lift-off.

It sometimes helps to pull Uke closer on to you if, for this throw anyway, you release your right hand from the orthodox grip on his left lapel and slide it up to take hold of the back of his collar.

KOSHI-WAZA

O-goshi is an ideal throw for the beginner as, in a comparatively simple fashion, it provides an introduction to the basis of all hip techniques — that is, the art of turning in with bent knees to make contact with an opponent.

Note carefully that when you execute o-goshi, your opponent falls off your hip and not off your back. What cannot be shown in a still photograph is how, at that stage of the throw, you jerk your right hip so that your opponent is almost shaken off, rather than thrown.

Uki-ogoshi (floating hip throw) is very similar in execution to o-goshi, the differences being that you do not drive your hip so deeply round into your opponent's stomach and do not raise, or jerk, your hip. The momentum for uki-ogoshi comes more from a twist of your bent body.

1 From a natural right-side posture, Tori pulls on Uke's outstretched left arm and breaks Uke's balance to his right front corner. At the same time, Tori's right foot is ready to cross to a position opposite the inside of Uke's left foot so that Tori will be able to pivot round. It is at this point that Tori may have difficulty releasing his right arm from Uke's sleeve grip in order to slip it around Uke's back.

2 Tori has released his right arm from Uke's sleeve grip and wrapped it firmly around Uke's back. While pivoting, Tori leans forward to begin raising Uke up on to his toes.

3 Tori bends forward, pulling with his right arm on Uke's back and continuing to pull Uke's right arm strongly from right to left over his shoulder and across his chest. Uke is lifted clear of the mat as the pulling action continues and Tori jerks his right hip to complete the throw.

Wrap your right arm firmly around your opponent's back and pull him strongly on to you to establish maximum body contact.

You may experience difficulty in moving your right hand away from your opponent's left lapel to do this as he is probably (and properly) gripping your right sleeve with his left hand.

4 Tori has pulled right through, shaking Uke off his right hip to land in front of him where he continues to control his opponent by retaining a sleeve grip.

To free your right arm, let go of his left lapel. Swing your right arm vigorously downward and outward beneath his left arm, then up on the outside and over the top of his elbow to reach inside his upper arm and beneath his armpit. This action should lock his elbow, cause him to let go of your sleeve and allow you to slip your right arm through his armpit and round on to his back.

It is permissable to grasp the back of your opponent's jacket or even his belt at the moment of throw if your require extra leverage to execute the technique.

TACHI-WAZA

Another of Judo's more dramatic techniques, ushiro-goshi is sometimes referred to as the back hip or rear loin throw. Like yoko-wakare (side separation) it can be a useful counter to any attacker positioning himself for a hip throw of almost any sort — provided that you are quick enough to spot him and make the early counter move! It does require the combination of good timing and some strength to perform ushiro-goshi properly and with confidence, but once perfected it can provide a quick and decisive counter-attack in a contest.

1 Tori has foiled Uke's turn into attack. He has stepped his left leg behind Uke's left leg and pivoted so that his body can bend forward to face in the same direction as that of Uke. Simultaneously Tori's right arm reaches across the front of Uke's body, to grasp Uke's left sleeve. Tori's left arm is gripping the back of Uke's belt or jacket.

2 Tori now has a firm grip of Uke and his legs straighten as he rises from a bent posture to lift Uke up on to his left front hip.

3 Tori straightens up and flicks his hip to throw Uke off and down on to the mat.

Maximum effect is derived from this technique if your timing is correct from the outset, so that the energy of your own counter-attack combines with that of your opponent to make the powerful lift as swift and effortless as possible.

4 Tori has retained contact with Uke during the execution of this technique and can now continue with groundwork.

When you crouch initially, use your encircling arms to hug your opponent's hips tightly to your chest. He will realize instantly that his attack has been blocked, and it is the instant when he tries to turn out that you can harness his energy to your own and go for the lift. Only experience can define this point of action. It will need practice — as will getting to know the moment at which you throw an opponent off and step back so that he does not land on your own legs or feet.

KOSHI-WAZA

Utsuri-goshi can be one of the most spectacular Judo techniques but it can be a real mess when attempted in a contest by someone not sufficiently skilled or strong to make it work. It is basically a counter-throw and it can be used to good effect by the proficient performer against attacking hip techniques.

Obviously, a certain amount of strength is involved in utsuri-goshi (as well as perfect timing) and therefore it is not advisable to attempt it against much heavier opponents or, in fact, against those taller than yourself. It is ideal for use against those slightly shorter than yourself, enabling you to bend your knees and get your hips well underneath theirs before making the lift.

1 Both are in a natural right-side posture when Tori, by bending his knees has blocked Uke from executing a hip technique and taken a strong hold around Uke's waist with his right arm.

2 Tori stands straight up and, with some arm lift to help, flips Uke up into the air off his right hip. At the same time Tori is stepping forwards with his right foot in preparation for turning the hip.

To make this counter-throw most effective it is essential to thrust your hips well up and forward when straightening your knees in order to maximize the initial lift.

3 Twisting to his right, Tori has continued to pull hard with his right hand around Uke's waist. This causes Uke to turn in mid-flight so that he lands stomach down on Tori's right hip.

While leaning backwards from the waist in order to thrust with the hips, care must be taken to retain balance as the weight of your opponent's body changes direction and swings down on to your hip.

4 Tori continues with a push-and-pull arm action and flicks his right hip to throw Uke off with what is (in itself as part of the whole technique) basically an o-goshi. Uke lands in front of Tori and the technique is complete.

KOSHI-WAZA

Often a beginner's instinct is to grapple an opponent around the neck in an attempt to start some sort of wrestling. However, in koshi-guruma the encircling arm of the attacker is not squeezed or used for any choking or strangulation upon the defender; in fact it can actually go under your opponent's armpit on to his back (as demonstrated in the photographs), or more across the top of his shoulders and behind his neck than wrapping around it. The arm is then used to bind the upper part of his body against yours. The extra high point of pulling power it provides helps you to lift your opponent diagonally across his extended hip.

1 From a natural right-side posture Tori turns in on his opponent, gripping Uke's outer upper sleeve and pulling it to break Uke's forward balance. Tori's right hand has left Uke's lapel and his right arm begins to encircle Uke's waist (or the back of his collar). Tori's right foot prepares for a pivot.

2 Tori's left foot swings round behind him and he pivots so that both feet are between Uke's feet facing forwards. Tori will drive his hips across Uke's body so that his right hip almost projects beyond Uke's right hip. Tori will continue to pull Uke's right arm tightly around his body while his right arm pulls Uke on to him. Tori bends forward and Uke's feet are about to leave the mat.

3 Tori continues to lift and pull Uke across his back. He straightens his bent knees and throws Uke over his hip on a large circular route to complete the throw.

4 Uke lands on the mat in front of Tori, who retains his grip on Uke's right arm.

As with all hip throw techniques, turn in low with both knees well bent so that you will have plenty of extra leverage as you straighten them to raise your opponent's feet clear of the mat.

In this particular hip throw it is essential to move your body well across that of your opponent, so that your leading hip eventually sticks out beyond the line of his body.

KOSHI-WAZA

In this variation of the basic o-goshi (major hip throw) the attacker moves in and makes a deliberate attempt to grab the back of his opponent's jacket or belt as an aid to hoisting him up and executing the technique.

There are two forms of tsuri-goshi. Kotsuri-goshi (small hip throw) is performed when you pass your encircling arm beneath your opponent's left armpit as in the basic o-goshi. The other form, demonstrated here, is otsuri-goshi (large lifting hip throw), and when executing this you pass your encircling arm right over your opponent's left shoulder in order to grasp the back of his belt or the far shoulder. The latter technique is really suitable for use only when faced with a much shorter opponent or with an opponent who fights from a very crouched stance.

1 From a natural right-side posture, Tori pulls on Uke's outstretched right right arm to break Uke's balance to the right front corner. At the same time, Tori's right foot is in readiness to pivot.

2 Tori has swung his left foot round behind him and pivoted on his right foot so that both feet now face forward in the same direction as Uke's. In turning, Tori has packed his body firmly against that of Uke. His knees are slightly bent and his right arm has passed around Uke's left shoulder to take hold of the right shoulder of Uke's jacket. Tori's left hand pulls Uke's right arm firmly around his own body and, as he leans forward, Uke is raised on to Tori's hips.

3 Tori completes the throw by simultaneously straightening his legs as he pulls to his left with both hands and finally twists his hips so that Uke travels around him in a circular route.

4 Uke break-falls in front of Tori, who still holds on to his opponent's right arm.

Apart from the movement of your encircling arm, everything said about o-goshi on page 50 also applies to tsuri-goshi.

With tsuri-goshi your encircling arm may reach around to grasp your opponent's belt. The further round you reach for a hold on the back of his belt or jacket, the more powerful will be your pull, lift and subsequent throw.

KOSHI-WAZA

Suki-nage is one of those opportunist techniques in which the surprise of attack initially provides an ingredient for success. Other requirements demanded of the attacker are expertise and a full commitment to the technique.

As in the application of most martial arts techniques, not only in Judo, he who hesitates is already lost when it comes to being committed to any form of attack. This technique is obviously ideal for strongly built players who have no doubt of their ability to perform the swift power lift required to execute the throw.

1 Starting from a natural right-side posture, Uke (on the right) has turned in, with knees bending, in preparation to execute a hip throw. In anticipation of this, Tori has bent his knees and lowered his hips so that his chest is about level with the back of Uke's hips, and he grips Uke's left sleeve.

2 Tori pushes strongly upwards to straighten his legs. As they straighten, he leans backwards. He retains his grip of Uke's left sleeve but his left hand (which is hidden from the camera) has let go of Uke's right sleeve to grasp hold of Uke and help with the high lift.

3 At the peak of this combined action, Uke is lifted well clear of the mat with his hips as high as possible up on to Tori's chest. Tori completes the technique by stepping backwards and allowing Uke to roll off him and drop on to the mat.

It has already been pointed out that suki-nage is an opportunist's technique which is not difficult to block and counter if caught halfway through its execution. However, the sort of circumstance under which this technique comes off most easily is when your opponent turns in on you, fails to perform and you catch him at just the moment when he is beginning to turn out from you.

4 As Uke lands on the mat, Tori still has hold of his jacket to control the direction of the fall and ensure that his opponent lands squarely on his back.

ASHI-WAZA

TACHI-WAZA

You will appreciate hiza-guruma as the perfect name for this throw once you have seen it properly executed. Your opponent literally pivots over your propping foot and is wheeled around in the air before landing.

Again, this is a technique in which timing is the key factor, superior weight or strength not being required to score with hiza-guruma. It is therefore another technique which can be employed usefully against bigger opponents, especially those who are taller than yourself.

Note also that this is a technique in which your leading foot makes firm contact with your opponent. You should, for the sake of both safety and effectiveness, ensure that you develop the art of turning your foot inwards so that contact is made with the sole of your foot and not the hard instep.

1 Tori and Uke are each in a natural right-side posture and Tori pulls Uke towards him. As Uke puts his right foot forward, Tori steps to Uke's left with his right foot and places it at a point almost opposite Uke's left foot. At the same time Tori pulls Uke to break balance at Uke's right front corner.

2 Now fully exposed to his right front corner, Uke begins stepping further forward with his right foot to retain balance. It is at this instant when Tori extends his left leg across Uke's right leg to place the sole of his left foot against the outside of Uke's right knee. Tori continues with his pull-and-push arm action.

3 Tori's final follow-through: he pulls Uke firmly around so that his body is pivoted from the point of his knee over Tori's propping left foot.

As with other leg and foot sweeping techniques, you can practise the main movement of hiza-guruma without a partner in order to perfect the art of retaining balance on your back foot while you lean slightly backwards to execute the actions of your swivelling arms and sweeping leg.

Always remember to curl your fist in towards you when grasping your opponent's lapel to assist in turning him to your left when making a throw from a natural right-side posture.

4 The throw is completed and Uke break-falls in front of Tori who retains hold of his left sleeve and stays in control of the situation.

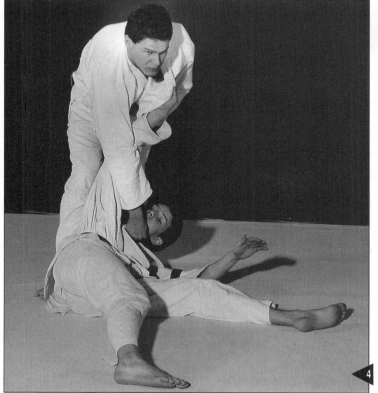

As with other techniques in which you are pulling your opponent round to break his balance to his right front corner, you should begin with the elbow of your pulling arm held high. Remember that you are pulling your opponent round, not trying to drag him downwards at that early stage.

The sort of opponent you are likely to catch with this technique is one who comes towards you with straight legs to begin with. Conversely, if you generally keep your own knees slightly bent when moving around opposite your opponent, you are less likely to be caught yourself with hiza-guruma.

TACHI-WAZA

O-uchi-gari is an opportunist technique which can be applied when your opponent is moving in almost any direction, especially if you perfect it for both right and left-sided attacks (that is, to clip the inside of your opponent's left leg with your own left leg, or his right leg with your right leg).

O-uchi-gari is also easy to combine with other techniques as well as proving useful in counter-attacks or combination throws.

It is obviously best employed when standing at fairly close quarters when your opponent cannot always see in which direction your feet are moving. It is certainly not very effective to attempt an o-uchi-gari from long range with outstretched arms.

1 Tori (on the left) begins the movement from a natural right-side posture but with his left foot pointing to his own left side. Tori begins moving his right foot to his left in order to provoke Uke into stepping forward with his own left foot.

2 In addition, Tori encourages Uke to move his left foot forward by breaking Uke's balance to the left front corner and then changing to a backward thrust. Immediately before Uke puts his left foot down, Tori also changes the direction of his right foot and slips it, with toes pointed downwards, behind the inside of Uke's calf.

3 Tori continues to slip his right leg in deeper until the back of his knee is touching that of Uke, then in one continuous movement Tori sweeps his right leg backwards and upwards to scoop Uke's left leg up in the air. Uke is unbalanced on his right leg and falls to his rear.

You must be standing fairly close in to your opponent to be able to execute this technique properly.

Point your toes down when executing the scoop and, while performing this off your left leg, don't pivot too far round to your left or you will soon be off balance (or vice versa if performing o-uchi-gari off your right supporting leg).

4 Simultaneously, Tori has driven off his left foot and pushed with his arms to force Uke backwards so that Uke lands on his back, perhaps slightly to his left rear corner.

As you push your opponent backwards with your right hand, it is helpful to draw the left lapel it is holding across your opponent's throat so that your forearm rests on his chest and improves the strength of your thrust.

TACHI-WAZA

Osoto-gari has become one of the most common techniques to be seen applied in Judo clubs today. It is particularly appealing to beginners who find that they can use it effectively — at least, against their peers — without having to make the effort of turning in on their opponents as demanded by most of the major throwing techniques. Unfortunately, many beginners can soon make a bad habit out of osoto-gari unless curbed and encouraged by their sensei into more adventurous techniques. On the other hand, it is a joy to behold an osoto-gari being executed cleanly and crisply by a judoka who has the technique properly perfected. It is particularly useful against an opponent who moves in quickly towards you.

1 Tori (facing the camera) has begun in a natural right-side posture and he breaks Uke's balance towards Uke's right back corner by gripping Uke's right sleeve with his own left hand and pulling sharply outwards and downwards. At the same moment Tori takes a grip either on Uke's left lapel, or the back of his collar with his right hand and pushes hard towards Uke's right shoulder.

2 Uke automatically raises his left foot to steady himself as his balance is broken towards his right back corner and Tori bends forward to place his right leg behind Uke's right leg.

3 Tori has pushed his right leg past the outside of Uke's right leg and curls it behind Uke's leg. As he continues to force Uke downwards and backwards, he straightens out his right leg and sweeps it up strongly behind him, so that he clips the inside back of Uke's right thigh with the back of his own right thigh to make Uke's legs fly up in the air.

While using your arms to break your opponent's balance towards his right back corner, lean forward so that the right side of your chest makes strong contact with that of your opponent. Continue with this upper body movement, bowing forward as though driving your head towards the mat as your leg sweeps up behind you.

4 Although only one leg is swept away, both of Uke's feet will be off the mat before he comes down with Tori pulling through strongly with his left hand and pushing with his right to complete the throw. Note how Tori has retained his own balance and kept a firm grip on Uke's sleeve to assist the break-fall or in case there is a need to follow up with groundwork or an arm-lock.

While your leg appears to be doing all the work, don't forget the important part both your hands are playing to help break your opponent's balance and enable you to perform this technique properly.

ASHI-WAZA

Sasae-tsurikomi-ashi is another sweeping technique but one which requires possibly a more vigorous arm action than some as you pull through to propel your opponent through the air right across the line of your own body to land on the mat almost behind your original position. However, the technique is basic and simple. It is particularly effective against an over-energetic opponent who might attempt to pull and drag you wildly around the mat without much regard for his own balanced footwork. As is the case with most ashi-waza (foot and leg techniques), sasae-tsurikomi-ashi can be useful for combining with other techniques such as osoto-gari.

1 From a natural right-side posture, Tori pulls on Uke's right sleeve w th his left hand and pushes Uke's left lapel across Uke's chest to break and his opponent's balance to his front right corner.

2 Tori pivots so that he is facing almost to his left side as the curled sole of his left foot smacks against Uke's right leg at a point near the bottom side of the sh n. Tori his continuing with the push-and-pull arm action, breaking Uke's balance to the front right corner.

3 Tori sweeps through with his left leg to remove Uke's feet from the mat, completing the throw with a simultaneous roundwards and downwards arm action which carries Uke into the air and over Tori's own left leg.

It is possible to execute sasae-tsurikomi-ashi from either left or right sides without the need to change the position of your grip and therefore alert your opponent to expect an attack from a particular posture.

4 Tori promptly brings his sweeping left leg back into position so that he is standing firmly and well-balanced on two feet as Uke lands in front of him.

Take your own weight firmly on your right foot as you make the sweep. The effectiveness of your sweep, and therefore the throw itself, will be improved if you can lean slightly backwards during this part of the action.

By pulling and pushing with a strong arm movement as you complete the turn, you will ensure that Uke falls clear of your own sweeping leg as it is brought back down on to the mat and the retention of your balance is not impaired.

ASHI-WAZA

Ashi-guruma can sometimes be mistaken for o-guruma (major wheel). The main difference between the two techniques is in the exact positioning of your sweeping leg across that of your opponent. In ashi-guruma your attacking leg goes across your opponent's leg as near as possible to his kneecap. In o-guruma your attacking leg is placed higher up against the front of your opponent's upper thigh, or even his lower abdomen. A strong arm action and swivelling of your body, though, is common to the success of both techniques.

1 Preparing for a right-sided attack, Tori's arms draw Uke towards him. Tori prepares to pivot on his own right foot which is now almost opposite Uke's left foot. He continues pulling with his arms to break Uke's balance.

2 Tori has brought h s left foot around-behind him and pivoted round to h s left, to be positioned almost cn the spot now vacated by h s right foot. As Tori switches the position of his feet, his right leg is swung upwards ard backwards to press against Uke's right knee.

3 With his head turning to look in the direction of the intended throw, Tori completes the throw with a strong arm pull-through which combines with the twisting of his upper body to pivot Uke over his right leg and through the air.

4 As Uke lands in front of Tori, Tori's-attacking leg has lowered and he stands well balanced on both feet, retaining a grip on Uke's right arm.

Try in this technique to perfect the art of striking your opponent's leg at a point just below his knee with your sweeping leg. The hard contact of a sweeping leg against a kneecap itself can be injurious, especially if your opponent is silly enough (and some are!) to come walking in towards you on straight, stiff legs. Apart from preventing such injury, slightly bent legs lower a judoka's centre of gravity and provide a good defence against attacks in general.

ASHI-WAZA

Harai-tsurikomi-ashi is a technique which, when used by beginners in early contest or randori situations, can easily become reduced to little more than a series of wild, frantic and dangerous kicking actions. Such beginners are under the misguided impression that they are influencing referees, judges, sensei or even their opponents with their lively aggression. Nothing could be further from the truth, however. If they achieve anything, it will be a penalty award from a referee, or a severe warning from their instructor or perhaps even a winning countersweep from their opponent.

As with many such techniques, the best approach is to settle down and study harai-tsurikomi-ashi very carefully. Rehearse it slowly and step by step with a partner to perfect accuracy of timing and point of contact. Speed and subtlety will come by themselves in good time.

1 Tori (on the right) steps forward, using mainly his hands on Uke's right sleeve and left lapel to force his opponent to break balance to the right back corner.

2 Tori pivots towards the left on his right-foot bringing Uke upwards and towards him. Simultaneously, Tori's left leg is extended across both of Uke's legs and the left foot curled inwards as the sole strikes Uke's ankle just above the instep of a foot now raised on tip-toe.

3 Pulling and pushing with his arms and continuing to twist, Tori uses the foot of his outstretched leg as a point of fulcrum over which Uke's legs sweep into the air.

4 Uke is thrown in a circular motion on to his own left side and he breakfalls on front of Tori.

Some instructors may chose to teach beginners a simpler form of harai-tsurikomi-ashi. In the simpler form you advance your left foot first in the normal way to force your opponent to retreat, first with his left foot and then with the right. As his right foot retreats, you follow up instantly with your own left foot and then quickly put your right foot alongside it. You are then able to sweep with your left leg before your opponent's right leg actually touches the mat.

If it is used properly, there is nothing wrong with this short-cut technique.

ASHI-WAZA

Deashi-barai can be a quick and surprising way of throwing your opponent on to the mat, provided that you manoeuvre him into a position in which his right foot (or left, if you are attacking his other side) is advancing towards you. If you are alert to the suprise potential of this technique, you can sometimes apply it to an opponent who is just too casual about taking up his first hold on you as you come together after hajime (begin) has been called. Grab your opponent's outstretched sleeve quickly and pull hard to make him stagger forward on to, say, his right foot. Whisk your left-hand grip on his right sleeve in a circular right-to-left motion at the same as time you sweep with your left foot on to his right ankle and you might flip him into the air without either of you having made any further body contact.

1 From a natural left-side posture Tori (facing the camera) begins by pushing Uke backwards. Then, as Uke resists and counter-pushes, Tori immediately pulls him further forward to Uke's left side. Uke prepares to put his left foot forward to retain balance. Tori transfers his own weight on to his left back foot and his right foot is in readiness to come alongside Uke's left foot and for the sweep.

2 Tori continues to break Uke's balance to the left. Tori's weight is now firmly on his left foot and the sole of his right foot curls inwards as it sweeps to contact the outside of Uke's left ankle.

3 Tori has followed through with a powerful right-leg sweep and continued to turn Uke's body with a left-and-right arm swivel action.

As with certain other techniques, you can practise the basic deashi-barai movements without a partner. On your own you can perfect the art of retaining balance on your back foot (right and left) while performing the pull-and-push action of the arms at the same time as you make a powerful leg sweep.

4 Both Uke's legs have flown into the air as Tori retains his own balance on that left back foot before Uke break-falls in front of him.

Perfect also the ability to turn your striking foot inwards so that it is the sole that makes contact with your opponent's ankle. Don't develop the bad habit of striking with the bony top of your instep, or simply kicking sideways at your opponent's outer shin bone: both actions not only make the technique ineffective, but also cause unnecessary bruising and sometimes more serious injury.

ASHI-WAZA

Kouchi-gari is a deceptively diminutive name for a technique which can be used with great scoring effect in randori or contest situations. It can be employed with equal effect in either left- or right-sided attack, depending upon which direction your opponent is moving in. It can also become part of a combination of techniques, and can be used as a feint, but is in itself a technique which is not very easy to counter. Kouchi-gari is quick and simple, but requires practice and timing to be either effective or to appear effortless.

1 From a natural right-side posture Tori pulls on Uke's right sleeve to break balance towards Uke's right front corner. This provokes Uke into stepping forwards on his right foot and simultaneously Tori steps back on his own left foot.

2 The instant before Uke puts his full weight down on that advancing right foot, Tori changes direction and pushes Uke backwards with both hands. At the same time Tori curls his own right foot so that his little toe skims across the mat and the sole of his foot strikes the back of Uke's right heel.

3 By now, Uke is spread-legged and off-balance as Tori's right foot moves to sweep Uke's right foot clear of the mat. Tori is pushing strongly off his own left foot and Uke is forced to fall to his rear.

When sweeping with your attacking foot, ensure that it is turned well inwards so that (as with most foot techniques) it is your sole that makes contact with the back of your opponent's heel. The action is a 'scoop' and not a 'kick'. Remember also that the little toe of that sweeping foot should remain skimming the mat as you follow through with the sweep. Keeping your foot low in this manner will help ensure that you push your opponent's leg along in the direction in which it is already moving, and not up into the air.

Try to avoid too much body twist as you curl your leg to fit your foot behind your opponent's heel; otherwise you may have difficulty retaining your own balance when completing the action as your attacking foot is returned to its normal position for a standing posture.

4 The throw is completed and ideally-Tori should finish clear of Uke's legs looking downwards on to his opponent before going into groundwork.

ASHI-WAZA

Like o-uchi-gari, kosoto-gari is a technique most usefully employed when an opponent comes in to you at close quarters. It is also a useful counter to a number of techniques, or as part of a combination follow-up to any of your own first-time attacks which may have failed. It can also be a useful surprise technique when applied swiftly to the type of swashbuckling opponent who swaggers forward to grab your jacket with some peculiarly individual type of stylish, but legal, grip. Like o-uchi-gari, kosoto-gari is a technique which can often be slipped in with alarming speed and accuracy by a judoka cool enough to keep his head when being harassed by an over-energetic opponent.

1 From a natural right-side posture Tori pulls Uke towards him, provoking Uke to step forward with his left leg. At this instant Tori immediately pushes back towards Uke's left rear corner and raises his own right foot in readiness for the reaping action.

2 Tori continues to push with his left-hand on Uke's right sleeve and pull with his right hand on Uke's lapel while swivelling slightly to his own right on his right foot. As he turns, Tori places the curled-in sole of his left foot against Uke's left heel.

3 Tori continues to turn Uke off balance with maximum use of arm action and follows through to throw Uke to the mat after clipping his opponent's heel with a strong upward sweep of his right leg. The combination of Tori's turning power from his arms and that of his leg sweep results in Uke's legs being taken from under him so that he flies into the air and break-falls in front of Tori.

The pull-and-push action of your right and left hands in this technique is a little bit like steering the wheel of a car.

The steering-wheel action of your hands and the sweep of your foot must be synchronized in order to achieve a perfect kosoto-gari. You can usefully 'shadow-box' this action by yourself without a partner, practising these arm and leg actions while retaining your balance.

Although a type of kosoto-gari attack can sometimes be launched from a long range, its effective surprise element comes about if you are close in to begin with and step smartly to the side of your opponent to make the sweep.

ASHI-WAZA

Kosoto-gake was at one time regarded as no more than a variation of ko-soto-gari but it is now considered to be an individual technique in its own right.

Kosoto-gake is an ideal follow-up to any kosoto-gari (minor outer reaping) attack which may have failed. In such a case, you would change the direction of your pull as you lower your sweeping leg to hook it around that of your opponent, and then push him backwards.

Like kosoto-gari, kosoto-gake can be applied with equal ease in either right- or left-handed attacks without first having to signal your intent by a change of grip on your opponent's jacket.

1 From a natural right-side posture Tori uses both hands to pull Uke towards him so that Uke is forced to step forwards on his right foot.

2 Just before Uke places his full weight on that advancing right foot, Tori changes his direction of attack and pushes of his own right foot to force Uke off balance to his right back corner. Tori helps this by pushing downwards and backwards on Uke's left sleeve and vigorously pushing Uke's left lapel with his right hand. Simultaneously Tori's left foot is raised and curled inwards and begins to move around the outer side of Uke's right calf.

3 Tori continues the hooking motion of his left leg so it will eventually carry Uke's right foot across the front of his own left leg. At the same time Tori will continue with the pushing action of both his hands in a right-to-left twisting action which will spiral Uke on one leg as he falls to his left back corner.

From whichever side you launch kosoto-gake, be careful to retain your balance on the foot remaining on the mat. Then, as your arm action helps turn the spiralling body of your opponent, twist the top half of your own body in the direction of the throw and look down towards the area of the mat on which he will land.

4 Tori retains his balance by swiftly returning his own sweeping (or hooking) leg to its normal position as he follows through with his arm action to deposit Uke in front of him on the mat.

Resist the temptation, which seems to come to those executing ankle techniques in particular, to launch your attack from too far out. While pulling your opponent towards either the right or left side, make sure that he is also drawn close in towards you.

ASHI-WAZA

Uchi-mata is a popular technique used frequently in both randori and contest situations. It is strong and effective if applied properly, but one of the main difficulties you will experience is being able to pivot round and retain balance on one supporting leg during the execution of so powerful a movement. That is why the timing of your uchi-mata attack in relation to the correct positioning of your opponent's body weight is most important.

Once mastered, particularly if perfected for use on both left and right sides, a good uchi-mata can be a real winner. Apart from that, though, it is useful for combination with other techniques.

1 Tori has spun Uke off balance to the right front corner and swung his left foot from its natural right-side posture to a spot behind his right foot and pointing outwards. Tori slides his right hand under Uke's left armpit to grasp the back of the collar and pull Uke towards him.

2 As Uke is raised forward Tori turns to his own left and with almost a spring, he turns to plant his left foot in place of his right foot (but pointing forwards). Simultaneously he sweeps his right leg backwards.

3 As Tori completes his about-turn by pivoting on his left foot, he simultaneously gets extra lift by straightening his left supporting leg, completes the backwards and upwards sweep of his right leg and jerks his right hip. These actions, all combined with Tori's strong arm action and revolving body movement, propel Uke through the air in a circular route.

Moving your grip to a position behind Uke's neck enables you to pull the upper part of his body more positively forwards as you begin to bend downwards and sideways.

At the point of making the throw effective, bend forwards low as if to drive your own head towards the mat and carry your sweeping leg backwards as high as possible. This makes your hips the fulcrum of a see-saw action.

4 Uke has been pulled round in almost a complete circle to break-fall in front of Tori who is able to maintain balance and full control over Uke by retaining a grip on his right sleeve.

Without a partner, you can practise the art of retaining your balance throughout this action, perhaps with the support of a chair back.

A bent supporting leg which is straightened out to provide maximum lift at the crucial moment is essential for an effective uchi-mata.

TACHI-WAZA

Osoto-guruma is basically the same as osoto-gari (major outer reaping) with the obvious difference, of course, that in this throw both your opponent's legs are swept away, not just the one as in osoto-gari.

Many beginners practising osoto-gari frequently make the mistake in randori or at gradings of sweeping both their opponent's legs away before they have even heard of this throw called osoto-guruma. More often than not, this two-legged 'mistake' comes about quite naturally if a judoka has stepped in too far with the leading foot to be able to sweep neatly at only the single leg nearest to him, or swept his attacking leg out at too wide an angle.

1 In a natural right-side posture Tori breaks Uke's balance towards Uke's right back corner by pulling on Uke's right sleeve sharply downwards and outwards with his left hand. Simultaneously Tori has gripped Uke's rear collar and is pushing towards Uke's right shoulder. Tori begins to raise his right leg.

2 Tori bends forward with his left foot placed to the outside of Uke's right foot. With knee raised and foot pointing downwards, Tori pushes his right leg forwards, past the outside of Uke's right leg.

3 Tori has pushed his right leg past the outside of Uke's right leg and as he continued to force Uke downwards and backwards with his arms, he straightened out his right leg behind him so that it reached across to clip the back of Uke's left leg. Tori's leg sweep has followed through to take both Uke's legs up into the air and deposit him on to the mat.

Everything explained about osoto-gari applies to osoto-guruma apart from the need to reach across your opponent's far leg with your sweeping leg. Your sweeping leg, with toes pointed, should strike your opponent's leg at a point just above the back of his knee. Your opponent's near-side leg should be raised up on the top of the thigh of your sweeping leg.

4 As Uke's legs fly into the air, Tori forces his own head down towards the direction in which Uke was to land, controlling his opponent with strong arm action and being perfectly positioned to follow through with kesa-gatame (scarf hold).

Osoto-guruma is useful against an opponent who might tend repeatedly to push and walk round to, say, your right side; it can also be employed to counter his own attempt at osoto-gari.

TACHI-WAZA

At first o-guruma may seem to the beginner to be similar to harai-goshi (sweeping loin). However, the main difference is that in o-guruma the technique is effected by use of the legs and not the hips as in harai-goshi.

There is in fact a closer relationship between o-guruma and ashi-guruma (leg wheel). Both of these techniques depend upon the effective use of a straight-legged rear sweep. In ashi-guruma, however, this sweeping leg makes contact with the opponent around the kneecap. In o-guruma the leg sweeps up higher to contact the top of an opponent's thigh or even the lower abdomen.

1 Tori pulls on Uke's right sleeve with his left hand in a circular motion and pushes with his right hand to break his opponent's balance to the front corner. At the same time Tori positions his right foot forwards at a point in front of the centre between Uke's feet and prepares to pivot.

2 Pulling and pushing with his arms, Tori pivots on his right foot, turning to his left, and brings Uke's body in towards him. His left foot has swung round smartly to replace the right, and his right leg is swung upwards and backwards across Uke's right thigh.

3 Uke has now been hoisted across Tori's hips. His feet have left the mat and as Tori pulls him around so does Tori's sweeping leg return to a balanced posture.

4 Tori's arms have finally pulled Uke round to fall on the mat in front of him and he is perfectly positioned to apply an arm-lock if necessary.

The combination of a quick pivot, switch of feet and a body twist with a strong pull on your opponent's right arm are important to the perfection of o-guruma.

As your outstretched leg sweeps up behind you, rock the top part of your body well forwards and downwards to get as much vigour as possible into the rocking, lifting action.

ASHI-WAZA

Okuri-ashi-barai differs from deashai-bari mainly in that your opponent is first taken off balance to his side rather than being drawn forwards on to an advancing foot. The effect of successful okuri-ashi-barai can therefore be more spectacular if a hard follow-through with your sideways leg sweep has a knock-on effect towards your opponent's other foot; then, both his feet will be taken into the air together. The technique also differs from deashibari in that it does not require your opponent to be moving towards you.

Okuri-ashi-barai is another technique in which timing is of the essence and it therefore has a good chance of being effective against heavier and taller opponents.

1

2

1 Tori and Uke are both in a natural right-side posture with Tori moving from right to left and vice versa in step with his opponent's movements. Suddenly, Tori reverses his movements to pull hard on Uke's right sleeve with his left hand as he pushes Uke's left lapel hard across towards the right side of Uke's chest. As Uke's balance is broken sideways on to his right foot, Tori prepares for a wide movement with his own left foot.

2 Just before Uke can place his full weight on his right foot, Tori continues to move his left foot round so that the sole makes contact with the outside top of Uke's right ankle. Note how Tori's arms assist in breaking Uke's balance.

3 Tori's arms continue to push and pull as his left foot has followed through to sweep Uke's feet up into the air.

Okuri-ashi-barai is one more technique from which the major movements of arms and legs — the push and pull of the arms and the simultaneous sweep of a leg — can be repeatedly practised without the need for an opponent. It is something you can incorporate into your warming-up routine when your first go on to the mat.

4 Tori has regained balance on both feet while retaining control of his opponent's arm as Uke breakfalls in front of him.

While your arms push and pull in a part-circular motion, your hips push forward so that your sweeping leg is in line with the top half of your body. Your foot is curled inwards so that it is the sole of your foot and not your bony instep which makes contact with the top of your opponent's ankle. The top half of your body leans slightly backwards in line with your sweeping leg, and at that point all your weight is balanced on your back foot.

MA-SUTEMI-WAZA

SUTEMI-WAZA

Tomoe-nage, generally referred to as the stomach throw but sometimes as the round throw, is a spectacular technique which most beginners often attempt at too early a stage in their judo career. It is one of a group of throws categorized as ma-sutemi-waza, which means rear body drop or sacrifice throws — the latter because, in order to perform the technique, you must sacrifice your own standing posture and go down on to the mat with your opponent. There, provided that you retain unbroken contact with him, you are permitted to carry on with groundwork techniques.

1 Tori and Uke are each in a natural right-side posture as Tori steps forward with his left foot to place it fairly deeply between Uke's feet. Note how Tori, in order to attain the most effective results from this throw, will next pull Uke forwards to begin breaking his balance to the front.

2 Tori keeps both elbows close into his chest and pulls Uke's upper body in towards him. At the same time, Tori will curl his back as he falls to the rear. He raises his right leg in a bent position to place his right foot against Uke's lower abdomen with the toes pointing outwards, away from the centre of his opponent's stomach.

3 Tori appears to slip beneath Uke's body as his curled back meets the mat and Uke's upper body is pulled down towards his chest, at which point Tori straightens his right leg to pivot Uke over his head.

Don't attempt this throw from a distance: you must step in close and deep between your opponent's legs with your leading leg.

You will only achieve the effective rocking action of this throw by pulling your opponent close in towards you as you fall to your rear and co-ordinating this with the extension of your throwing leg.

4 Uke break-falls, but is still controlled by Tori who has retained hold of his jacket in readiness to follow through into groundwork.

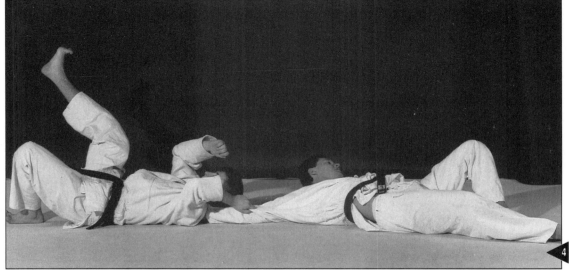

SUTEMI-WAZA

Ura-nage is another technique not normally found in syllabus work, but it is in nage-no-kata which the judoka will be expected to perform at some time on the way up through the grading system. As a kata technique, then, it is one you will practise with a partner during kata training sessions. If the mat is ever crowded, it is not recommended for use in randori as you cannot be sure that you will not throw your partner on top of another pair practising out of sight behind you and thus cause injury. Once you have successfully launched yourself and your partner into this powerful sacrifice technique, there is little or nothing you can do to control how or where he might land.

In a contest, ura-nage can be an effective block and counter-attack if you catch an opponent as he turns in to attack you with any hip technique.

1 Tori and Uke (facing the camera) each begin in a natural right-side posture. As Uke turns out from an attacking technique, Tori has stepped forward strongly with his left foot. Both knees are bent to lower his hips. At the same time, Tori's left arm has encircled Uke's body and he places a flat right hand on Uke's upper abdomen.

2 Tori slides both legs beneath Uke. He pushes forward with his hips to flip Uke into the air as his left arm pulls and his right arm pushes. His own body is thrust backwards.

3 Tori follows through with the action, falling backwards and twisting so that Uke falls across his left shoulder and clear of his own body.

Bent knees and vigorous hip movement are essential ingredients to make this technique effective.

It is permissible to get hold of your opponent's belt for greater lift and leverage when executing ura-nage, but release one of your arms (left or right, depending upon the direction in which you are throwing your opponent) in order to break-fall safely.

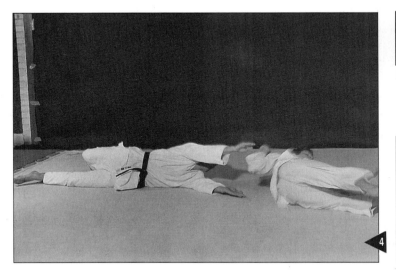

4 Tori break-falls backwards to hit the mat, just fractionally before Uke lands behind him.

This is one of the comparatively few occasions when you are likely to be throwing yourself backwards into a break-fall from a standing position, so remember to keep your head bent forward to avoid a whiplash bump on to the mat.

Sumi-gaeshi is exactly what it is called — a corner throw — because the technique begins by breaking an opponent's balance to a front corner and then following through with action which propels him over your head in that same corner direction.

Although the technique is demonstrated here with both judoka beginning in an upright stance, it can be particularly effective against an opponent who continually bends forward either through fatigue or a desire to pull his hips as far away from you as possible.

1 From a natural right-side posture Tori slips his right hand through Uke's left armpit to grasp Uke's jacket just behind the shoulder. Tori's left hand grabs Uke's right upper sleeve on the outside as he forces Uke to break balance to his right front corner and Uke's right leg steps forward.

2 Tori has stepped in deeply with his left-foot as though for tomoe-nage, and as he rolls backwards in the direction of Uke's right front corner, his right leg is raised to hook his right foot behind Uke's left knee or thigh. As the backward roll lowers his hips, he pulls Uke's upper body firmly down towards him.

3 Tori completes the throw by rolling backwards and simultaneously extending his right leg in a curling action which hooks Uke's legs up into the air.

You will get maximum power from this technique by beginning the hooking action of your leg at the same time as you begin to throw yourself backwards. These two actions must become synchronized as one simultaneous movement. Little will be achieved by rolling backwards and then trying to hook with your left leg.

More futile still are efforts by beginners who seem to be afraid of launching themselves backwards. When first attempting tomoe-nage, they often appear almost to sit down before applying the leg action. Only full and total commitment to the proper way of applying the technique will provide you with any chance of it being effective

4 Tori continues to complete the roll backwards, pulling down with his arms so that Uke rolls forwards to break-fall on his right shoulder. Tori releases his own right hand but retains his left-hand grasp of Uke's sleeve in readiness for groundwork.

YOKO-SUTEMI-WAZA

Yoko-gake, as well as being known as side dash, is also sometimes called side hook or side body drop. It is in the category of throws referred to as yoko-sutemi-waza (side sacrifice techniques) and in a contest provides a useful means of flooring an opponent with an apparent minimum of effort. It is also a sacrifice technique which the judoka will be expected to demonstrate as part of kata.

As a contest technique, yoko-gake can be applied from either right or left with equal facility. Timing is of the essence in a successful yoko-gake and it can therefore be effective against taller or heavier opponents. However, use it in a contest situation only if your are confident of being able to impose your authority should you not score Ippon, once you are both down on the mat.

1 Tori and Uke are each in a natural right-side posture when Tori pulls on Uke's right sleeve with his left hand and pushes Uke's lapel across Uke's chest with his right hand. This action breaks Uke's balance to his right front corner.

2 Tori curls the sole of his left foot and turns it inwards to place it firmly behind Uke's right ankle. He continues to move Uke off balance with his arms, pulling and pushing to Uke's right side.

3 Tori has swivelled on his right foot towards his own left side. He rolls sideways, downwards and backwards as he sweeps Uke's right leg away with his own left foot so that Uke begins to turn and fall.

As your leg sweeps sideways, bend on your supporting leg and roll sideways on to the mat rather than falling.

Your left arm, although doing all the pulling, should be tucked well into your left side. This not only maximizes the power of the pull, but also prevents your elbow from sticking out and possibly becoming injured during the rolling fall.

Remember to retain your hold on your opponent at the end of the throw.

4 Tori continues to roll on to his back as his strong and twisting arm action turns Uke into a break-fall alongside his own body.

YOKO-SUTEMI-WAZA

Yoko-otoshi is a sacrifice throw which depends for much of its success upon you being sufficiently quick and skilful with your initial feint before changing direction for the main attack. Once that has been achieved, your opponent's own weight and energy will (in true Judo fashion) have created much of the momentum required to topple him over your outstretched leg. Again, this is not recommended as a contest technique for those in any doubt of their ability to follow through with effective groundwork.

1 Both judoka face each other in a normal right-side posture when Tori pulls and pushes with his arms and takes half a step to his right as though to break Uke's balance in that direction.

2 As Uke resists, he pulls in the opposite direction (towards Tori's left side) and at that instant Tori changes direction also, pushing on Uke's left lapel with his right hand and pulling Uke's sleeve with his left hand. Simultaneously Tori prepares to drop his own hips in order to slip the calf of his outstretched left leg forward against the side of Uke's right heel.

3 Tori has made the drop and completes the throw by falling on to his own left side, at the same time shortening his arms to draw his opponent towards him and making Uke spiral sideways and downwards.

A surprise element is not the least of the requirements for success with yoko-otoshi, and even then only your total commitment from the outset will make it truly effective.

There must be no delay between changing the direction of your pull on your opponent, the breaking of balance and the sliding of a leg against his heel (or ankle). The three movements must become blended into a single snap combination, or he will guess what you are up to before your hips are half-way through their drop on to the mat.

4 Uke lands on the mat near to Tori who, having retained his grip, will will be able to continue with groundwork.

And while you are doing all this, don't forget the powerful contribution your arms can make.

Finally, when practising this throw, or any sacrifice technique, always follow through at the end by moving instantly into some form of groundwork. So many players practise sacrifice throws as independent techniques, unrelated to the opportunity for groundwork they can bring about. This often results in such players 'freezing' after having successfully executed a sacrifice throw in a contest and then losing the benefit of the advantage they have created.

YOKO-SUTEMI-WAZA

Tani-otoshi requires all the same basic skills as yoko-otoshi, but differs in its final execution and the position in which your opponent eventually lands on the mat. In tani-otoshi your opponent is thrown on to his side, but in yoko-otoshi he is thrown more on to a back corner shoulder. This, of course, comes about from the differing directions in which you slide your leg in against your opponent's foot.

1 Beginning from a natural right-side posture, Tori pulls with his arms and steps backwards to break balance at Uke's right front corner until Uke reacts by taking a step backwards with his right foot.

2 Tori immediately follows Uke's withdrawal movement, pushing on Uke's left lapel while pulling downwards and backwards on his right sleeve to break balance to Uke's right back corner. At the same time Tori has lowered his hips and slides his left leg straight out on to the mat by the outside edge of Uke's foot.

Every bit of commitment to this throw is no less than that demanded of you in the execution of the related yoko-otoshi.

In both techniques, there is the need to slide in deeply with your attacking leg. Your leading foot should be turned inwards and pointing, with your little toe just skimming the mat.

3 Tori drops himself quickly on to the mat, holding Uke close in and twisting to his left so that Uke almost tumbles over that outstretched leg and break-falls to his right rear corner. Tori has helped him on his way by moving his right hand grip on Uke's left lapel and giving him an upward lifting push beneath the left armpit.

4 Tori remains in control of the situation and in readiness for ground work almost before Uke's feet have landed on the mat.

This ensures that your leg will follow at the lowest possibly point against the ankle of your opponent and provide the most effective point of fulcrum over which he will topple.

YOKO-SUTEMI-WAZA

Although classified as a sacrifice throw, yoko-wakare can also be a useful counter to several popular forms of attack — o-goshi, seoi-nage or uki-goshi. In every case, though, success depends upon your anticipating the attack. You must be quick enough to step around your opponent's hips to take advantage of his own momentum as you drop to the mat to perform your own yoko-wakare.

1 From a natural right-side posture, Tori feints to his own right and then breaks balance to Uke's right front corner in readiness to spreadeagle his legs and slide his right leg along the outside of Uke's right foot. Tori pulls on Uke's right sleeve with his left hand and pushes Uke's left lapel with his right.

2 In a continuing action Tori has dropped his hips to the mat, pulling his opponent further down towards him as Uke begins to tip over the block of Tori's outstretched right leg.

3 Tori, now on his back, has continued spiralling to his own left and used his arms to wheel Uke through the air above and across his own body.

The sliding forward of your spreadeagled legs and your own body drop to the mat should be a simultaneous action. Don't sit down and then lean backwards — slide smoothly into your position on the mat and roll to your left as you do so.

If your 'prop' leg is in the correct position and your arm pull is strong, your opponent can do little other than begin to lean over you.

Additional impetus for that final swivelling lift you will need to propel your opponent through the air may be achieved by sliding your right handful of his left lapel up and under his left armpit. Straighten your right arm and shorten your left as he wheels around you and that will help turn him on to his back.

4 Uke is propelled by a pull-and-push-arm action over Tori's body to land on the mat more or less at right angles to his attacker who, in this action, has retained physical contact.

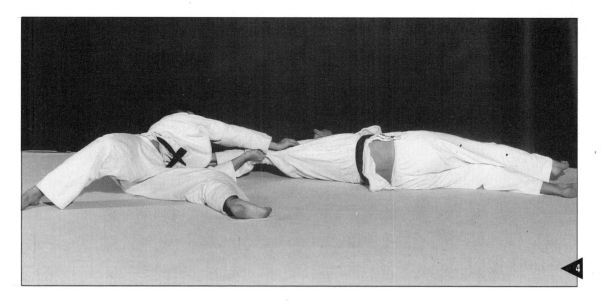

YOKO-SUTEMI-WAZA

Uki-waza is classified as a side body drop and is a sacrifice throw. Throughout the history of Judo, it has remained one of the sport's finest techniques and has been practised by many masters. Not usually a syllabus technique, uki-waza must be learned as part of kata, but it is generally useful to the judoka in contest situations.

The application of uki-waza is simply a matter of dropping backwards and sticking out a leg for your opponent to spiral over with an advancing foot. The difficulty is in achieving this apparently simple effect. To do so, you will require to perfect fine co-ordination and a good sense of your opponent's movement and point of balance. When perfected, uki-waza can be applied with ease from either left or right side without changing your grip on your opponent's jacket.

1 Tori and Uke are each in a natural right-side posture. Tori has feinted as though to break Uke's balance to Uke's left, and he suddenly changes direction to break balance to Uke's right front corner. As Uke steps his right foot forward to retain balance, Tori prepares to lower his hips and slide his left leg across the front of Uke's right foot.

2 Tori slides his left leg fully along the outside of Uke's right foot on the floor as he pulls on Uke's right sleeve with his left hand and pushes with his right hand on Uke's left lapel. At the same time, note how Tori is turning to his own left side and pulling Uke further off balance.

3 Tori's left arm is pulled down towards his own chest. His right arm extends and pushes as Uke is finally pivoted over the extended leg to begin turning into a break-fall.

As in the application of all sacrifice throwing techniques, any hesitation of commitment on your part can end in disaster, for if your attack is not swift and fully effective, you will lose the initiative and your opponent is the one who will end up with the advantage on the ground.

It is not always necessary to feint an off-balancing movement as suggested. You may have an opponent who is continually dragging you around in a circular pattern, in which case you simply wait until the instant his lead foot comes to the mat to drop your hips and slide your tripping leg across his path.

A vigorous steering-wheel action of your hands helps turn your opponent's toppling body through the air.

4 Tori holds firmly on to Uke's right sleeve with his left hand as Uke break-falls near his left shoulder and becomes vulnerable to a follow-up attack on the ground.

YOKO-SUTEMI-WAZA

SUTEMI-WAZA

Hane-makikomi is one of several throws based upon combining basic soto-makikomi with another technique — in this case hane-goshi. A careful analysis of the movements shows that the whole technique of hane-makikomi begins as for hane-goshi, but when you begin to turn, the start of the distinctive makikomi overarm action comes into play.

1 From his natural right-side posture Tori breaks Uke's balance to the right front corner. Next he will cross over with his right foot to pivot and drive his hip deep into Uke as for hane-goshi. Tori pulls Uke's right sleeve with his left hand, but his right has already taken a grip high on Uke's collar in readiness to be swung over Uke's head.

2 Tori's legs continue to move as for normal hane-goshi and as he leans forward, pulling on Uke's sleeve, Uke's feet begin to leave the mat. Tori's right arm has followed his body twist and is now almost ready for the final action.

Depending upon which side you are attacking from, there is a need to wrap your opponent's leading arm tightly around your body, so put plenty of pull on that arm as you pin it close to your twisting body.

Although your right arm can continue with its rounding, circular movement, it can finish up in one of two ways.

3 Tori completes the hane-goshi 'spring' part of the movement to throw Uke into the air, but continues to bend forward and round, driving his head down towards his own left side. Tori's right arm has passed through its swing over the top of Uke's left arm and followed round to add to the momentum of Uke's body revolving around him.

You can reach out and use your right arm to ease the break-fall or you can swing it in around your own body, and thus further pin your opponent's right arm beneath your right armpit.

4 Tori has thrown Uke with a round, winding movement and Uke's body drops sideways on to the mat where Tori, still retaining a grip, is free to continue with a groundwork attack.

YOKO-SUTEMI-WAZA

SUTEMI-WAZA

Yoko-guruma, sometimes know as side whirl, is another technique which the student judoka will come across in the kata but not necessarily in any grading syllabus. There is, however, a need to perfect this technique because yoko-guruma can also usefully be applied as a sacrifice technique during contests.

Yoko-guruma is a particularly effective counter-throw for use against an opponent attacking with osoto-gari, or any technique in which your opponent has to commit a leading leg, or gives you the chance to step around it.

1 From a natural right-side posture Tori pulls towards his own right on Uke's left lapel and pushes Uke's right arm in that direction in order to feint an attack towards Uke's left side.

2 As Uke resists by pulling back towards his own right side, Tori instantly changes his line of attack to that side also and steps strongly forwards to place his left foot firmly down on the outside of Uke's right foot. See how Tori's left hand is exploiting Uke's own momentum in that direction and is now pulling through on Uke's right sleeve towards Uke's right side.

3 With legs spread-eagled, Tori drops his hips and rolls towards his left side. Uke's own momentum helps Tori to pull Uke downwards and sideways.

For maximum effect in this technique pull your left arm (if applying a right-side technique, as illustrated) strongly downwards towards your own chest in order to achieve the maximum turning of your opponent's body.

4 Tori has shortened his left arm and pulled, while extending his right arm, to produce a swift and powerful arm action which propels Uke across Uke's right shoulder to land on the mat just clear of Tori's head.

KATAME-WAZA
GROUNDWORK TECHNIQUES

While there are, of course, differing circumstances under which it is applied, the same principle of exploiting an opponent's strength and direction of energy and using it towards his own defeat is just as important to katame-waza (general name for groundwork, or grappling techniques) as to nage-waza (throwing techniques).

Osae-komi-waza is the category of groundwork techniques concerned with grappling upon the mat so that your opponent becomes immobilized and held down.

To achieve this it is obvious that you must remain as Tori, the one in control of the situation the whole time.

Domination of the opponent beneath begins with your establishment and maintenance of maximum body contact, so that your full weight bears down upon him constantly. This includes periods during which you may be moving around or across his body in the course of changing techniques. Keeping your legs well away from being grabbed, your weight is best applied if forced forward and

down through contact with your upper rib cage on to, say, your opponent's chest if facing upwards or the back of his shoulders if face down. This leaves your arms free to apply strangles or control his limbs.

Even if you are the judoka underneath, you can still attack. In fact, attack and counter-attack is the best form of defence. While keeping calm, you should never remain still; always be ready to take the initiative by bridging and turning, groping for a strangle or the application of an opportunist's arm-lock.

The normal scarf hold, or hon-kesa-gatame, is the usual manner of applying this popular hold-down technique, although variations of it known as kuz-ure-kesa-gatame are in fairly common use. It is one of the most generally used hold-down techniques, probably because it is one of the most effective. Beginners are usually taught kesa-gatame fairly early in their Judo career and continue to employ it on appropriate occasions during randori, contests, gradings and, of course, during kata presentations.

1 With his left hand Tori grips Uke's right sleeve beneath the outside elbow to pull that arm clear of Uke's body and open up a space beneath Uke's right armpit. Tori drops to sit in that space. He tucks his right hip firmly against Uke's body and pulls Uke's right arm with his left hand close into his body and traps it beneath his own left armpit.

2 Simultaneously Tori's right arm encircles Uke's neck and he slips his thumb inside Uke's jacket to take a strong grasp of the collar almost over Uke's right shoulder. Tori bends forward, tucking his head well down and leaning heavily on to Uke's rib cage. The hold-down is secure.

Note how your head should be curled well down with your chin tucked in to foil any attempt which your opponent might make to counter-attack with a choke or strangle, if he ever managed to grasp your lapel.

You must push with your feet on to the mat to ensure that your hips are always driven close into your opponent's body.

However much your opponent struggles, you must retain your own position by shuffling on your bottom and sliding your legs into their original position. This will ensure that your trailing leg is always clear of becoming entangled and trapped by your opponent's swinging legs as he struggles.

OSAE-KOMI-WAZA

Ushiro-kesa-gatame is more than just a simple variation on the basic kesa-gatame in as much as the position of both participants in relation to one another is completely changed. It is a hold-down position which a judoka can easily find himself almost automatically rolling into while generally grappling with an opponent for some advantage on the ground.

Otherwise, there may be occasions when you are unhappy with the effectiveness of a straightforward hon-kesa-gatame from which your opponent may be in danger of escaping. Then you can transpose your leg positions and change to ushiro-kesa-gatame.

1 From the position of a normal hon-kesa-gatame Tori has spun around so that he is facing towards Uke's feet. Tori is now sitting behind Uke's right arm which is stretched backwards and across Tori's body. Tori holds it firmly in place by grasping and pulling on the underside of Uke's upper sleeve.

2 As Uke struggles, Tori leans heavily across Uke's chest to force his head down and places his left forearm on the mat alongside Uke's body or grips the left side of Uke's belt. Note how Tori's legs are spread to provide a wide base for maximum balance.

Lean heavily across your opponent's rib cage but keep your head bent well forward, chin tucked in and throat protected from any attempts which he might make to reach across your collar for a choke or strangle.

While it is more effective to keep your body high up across your opponent's chest, don't sit so far back that you impair his breathing with the back of your jacket.

Kata-gatame is a technique which you can often apply to an opponent who has not been securely pinned by, for instance, a kesa-gatame. Your movement from one position to another can be quite simple. An effective kata-gatame is a popular and proven technique used by judoka manoeuvring to control a heavier opponent on the ground.

In a contest you might easily find yourself applying kata-gatame with your legs spread on the mat as for kesa-gatame, but this is not by any means as effective as bending up on the right knee with hips raised and driving weightily down upon your opponent's shoulder.

1 Uke is lying face up when Tori moves in on his right side. Tori presses his right knee firmly up against Uke's right side as he raises Uke's right arm.

2 Tori leans forward to trap Uke's arm between the right side of his face and the right side of Uke's face. Tori's right arm bends Uke's arm towards Uke's left shoulder and encircles Uke's neck to take a grip at the back of his collar. Tori's left hand gives extra push against Uke's trapped arm and he drives in against Uke from an outstretched left leg.

Prevent your opponent from turning in towards you in an attempt to escape by keeping your bent right leg very firmly wedged against the side of his body.

As with kesa-gatame, keep your head bent well down and forward to reduce any opportunity which he might have to employ an escaping counter-move.

KAMI-SHIHO-GATAME *UPPER FOUR QUARTER HOLD*

Kami-shiho-gatame is applied in the course of groundwork if and when you find yourself above your opponent's head with his body lying face upwards and stretched out in a line with your own frontal direction. Very often, kami-shiho-gatame can be a follow-through technique to a tomoe-nage sacrifice throw; or it can be performed from a position you find yourself rolling into from an ineffective scarf hold or some other groundwork attack you have failed to press home hard enough to establish full control over your opponent. As with yoko-shiho-gatame, there are several variations to kami-shiho-gatame, the most common of which is kuzure-kami-shiho-gatame.

1 Tori kneels down above and in line with Uke's body which is lying face upwards.

2 Tori's arms pass beneath Uke's arms which are firmly pinned in place when Tori presses his weight down on Uke's body and tightens his grip at the waist on either side of Uke's belt. Tori's head is turned sideways and pressed firmly down on to Uke's upper abdomen. Uke's head turns sideways to facilitate breathing. Any attempt at bridging by Uke is countered by Tori extending his legs backwards and outwards so that, pushing off his toes, his weight is driven even harder into Uke's abdomen. The use of both legs simultaneously in this manner, or one at a time depending upon the direction of Uke's movements, helps Tori retain full control.

In kami-shiho-gatame, or any variation which requires you to spread your legs to provide pushing power when in a face-down position, always turn your toes into the mat. Apart from maximizing your pushing power off the foot or feet, it will save you from experiencing uncomfortable burns usually acquired when sliding a flattened instep around on the mat.

However, in this particular technique, it is essential that, while pushing off your toes, you keep your bottom low and flattened so that there is no space between yourself and your opponent's body.

It is possible that when grappling with an opponent you may find yourself quite unexpectedly straddling his chest and in a position to apply tate-shiho-gatame. Generally referred to in English as trunk holding, this technique is also sometimes called a straight four corner hold. Tate-shiho-gatame is not the ideal hold-down to attempt against a heavier or stronger opponent because of the likelihood of being rolled over. On the other hand, some lightweights who have worked hard to perfect this technique stick like limpets around their opponent's upper body and can use it effectively against all-comers.

1 On bent knees, Tori begins by straddling Uke's chest with both knees tucked in against Uke's ribs. Uke's arms raise up in defence.

2 Tori leans his weight down on to Uke's left shoulder, trapping Uke's extended left arm between his own head and that of his opponent. At the same time Tori has slipped his left arm around Uke's neck and grasps him tightly as Uke tries to throw him off by bridging or rolling. Note how strongly Tori's legs are clamped around Uke's body.

One danger in too much reliance upon this particular hold-down is that your opponent's legs are left free to provide a powerful contribution to any counter-attack.

Also, if you move your knees too high up your opponent's body, you will be top-heavy and vulnerable to being rolled over his head. You can prevent him rolling you off by driving the top of your own head into the mat by the side of one of his shoulders.

OSAE-KOMI-WAZA

In both yoko-shiho-gatame and its variant kuzure-yoko-shiho-gatame (broken four quarter hold) your body is initially placed at right angles to that of your opponent in order to apply the technique. The free movement of your legs to counter his struggles for freedom is of crucial importance.

Kuzure-yoko-shiho-gatame is a variation in which your left arm comes forward over your opponent's left shoulder to grip his belt at the rear. Your right hand grips behind his trouser leg, to control the rolling action of his attempts to escape.

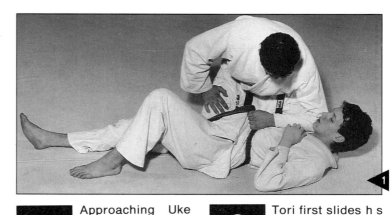

1 Approaching Uke from his right side Tori moves his knees in close to control Uke's body movement.

2 Tori first slides his left hand behind Uke's collar. Tori slips his right hand deep between Uke's legs and grasps the back of Uke's belt on the left side, or the bottom of his jacket if the belt cannot be reached. Tori's left hand has now passed over Uke's right shoulder to take a firm grip on the back of Uke's left side collar.

3 Tori's legs are now wide apart, feet raised on to the toes and driving his weight forwards and downwards on to Uke's body. His head is forced down on to the mat to prevent Uke from rolling away from him.

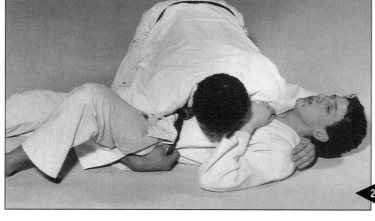

There's no hard-and-fast rule about the movement of your legs as you shift them in and out, together or singly: you can use whatever combination of movements is necessary to control the movements of your opponent.

In the basic yoko-shiho-gatame it is advisable, when you force your head and upper body hard down on to your opponent's chest, that you also turn your head sideways to face his head. Otherwise, he could reach out for an effective choke.

KANZETSU-WAZA

ARMLOCKS

Kansetsu-waza in competitive Judo are concerned only with the application of a limited variety of arm-locks — various methods of applying a reverse hold against the elbow joint. Any additional locks on legs, knees, ankles, wrists, spine, neck, fingers or toes, as well as direct reverse holds on shoulder joints, are not permitted because of the regard for safety in the sport.

As with shime-waza (strangle techniques) you must not play the hero too much, certainly in your beginner days. Tap in submission the instant you feel your opponent has applied the technique on you properly. If you are ever caught with both hands and arms trapped, tap on the mat with your feet or cry out — or do both.

The primary defence against kansetsu-waza, as with both shime-waza and osae-komi-waza, is to first sense your opponent's intentions and move quickly out of position before he can apply the technique.

UDE-GARAMI *ENTANGLED ARM-LOCK*

You don't have to look to closely at ude-garami and the shape it forms to understand why it is sometimes referred to as 'the figure four'. Ude-garami is generally demonstrated from the position shown here, in which you bend over your opponent's prostrate body to reach the far-side arm. With experience, though you will eventually find it possible to apply ude-garami from different postures and with some variations.

1 Kneeling, Tori approaches Uke from the right side and leans over his opponent's body. As Uke raises his left arm as though to grab Tori's jacket, Tori seizes the inside of Uke's left wrist with his own left hand, palm downwards and facing away from him. Tori has now pressed Uke's arm down so that the back of Uke's hand is on the mat. As Uke's arm bends at the elbow, Tori slips his right hand beneath Uke's upper left arm to grab the top side of his own left wrist.

2 Leverage against Uke's elbow joint is applied as Tori controls Uke's wrist with his left hand and pins Uke's right shoulder down with the weight of his body. Tori finally raises his own right elbow, which forces Uke's left elbow up away from the mat, and submission should follow.

Juji-gatame is sometimes referred to as 'the step-over arm-lock' because you step over your opponent's throat in the course of executing the technique. It is an ideal technique to be dropped into after you have thrown an opponent and then find it necessary, for whatever reason, to follow up immediately with a ground-work attack. It also fully demonstrates the desirability of always hanging on to one arm of your opponent after you have thrown him: it is from such a retained arm that you are ideally positioned to launch into juji-gatame.

1 With both hands Tori has grasped Uke's outstretched right arm at the wrist and pulled it upwards to raise Uke's right shoulder from the mat. Tori has slid his right foot deeply in between that shoulder and the mat, while his left foot has stepped over Uke's throat to a spot just above Uke's left shoulder.

2 With the back of Uke's straightened elbow already pulled in hard to Tori's groin and the whole of his opponent's arm trapped between his own legs, Tori has dropped backwards on to the mat at a right angle to Uke's body. Now Tori uses both hands to keep the inside of Uke's wrist facing upwards while he raises his hips to bend the back of Uke's elbow against his own groin. Tori's feet hold Uke firmly locked and a submission should follow.

UDE-GATAME *ARM CRUSH*

Ude-gatame is really just what the technique's English name implies — you hold your opponent's outstretched arm and crush the joint against your own body. A straight arm is an open invitation to an arm crush from almost any position, but ude-gatame is generally demonstrated, as here, with the defender lying face upwards and at a right angle to the kneeling attacker.

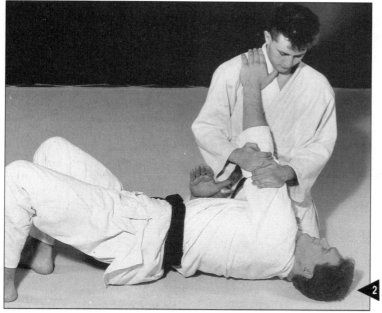

1 Lying down, face-up, Uke turns to his right and reaches over with a straight left arm as though to grab Tori who is kneeling.

2 Tori seizes the back of Uke's elbow with both hands and pulls the straight arm into his own body. Tori controls Uke's body by pushing his left knee on the mat close up to Uke's right chest and arm. Tori's right knee can be pushed against Uke's left armpit. As maximum pressure is applied against Uke's elbow joint, a submission should be achieved.

Hiza-gatame is perhaps more complicated than most kansetsu-waza as you have to co-ordinate several movements from different parts of the body. In many instances kansetsu-waza will start when your opponent is already on the ground and not standing as demonstrated here. Once on the mat, movements are exactly the same.

1 Tori (on the left) breaks Uke's balance to the front left corner and stretches out his right leg to place the sole of his right foot firmly against Uke's left knee.

2 Tori falls to his right rear corner, taking Uke with him. He pushes on Uke's left knee to flatten the leg on to the mat. Tori, rolling to his right side, continues with the orthodox grip on Uke's left lapel, or collar, and right sleeve. Note, though, how Tori's left knee is already raised towards Uke's outstretched right arm, Tori's left foot being planted against Uke's right hip to control Uke's body.

3 Tori completes the lock on Uke's right elbow by continuing to roll to his right so that he is looking towards the mat himself. Then, as his left hand applies pressure against Uke's right elbow, so does his left knee turn inwards to add pressure against the back of the elbow and achieve a likely submission.

KANSETSU-WAZA

Waki-gatame can be applied from either a groundwork situation as demonstrated, or from a standing posture.

From a normal right-side standing posture you would first grasp your opponent's raised right wrist, say, from underneath with your own right hand in a reverse grip and draw it towards you across the front of your own body. Simultaneously you would bend forward over the arm, pivot on your left foot and step back with your right. You would pass your left arm over the top of your opponent's outstretched right arm and sink your armpit on to the back of his elbow continuing exactly as shown in a groundwork situation.

1 In the course of grappling, Tori (on the left) has found himself in a position in which he has been able to clamp Uke's outstretched right arm at the elbow joint beneath his left armpit. Tori turns to his right as he sits on the mat with legs splayed more or less as for kesa-gatame.

2 Tori twists Uke's right wrist away from him, using both hands in order to keep Uke's elbow locked. At the same time Tori pulls the wrist in an upwards direction while bearing downwards with his armpit against Uke's elbow joint; a submission should follow.

While all shime-waza are generally referred to as strangles, some of them are actually chokes. In a strangle, the player's blood supply is cut off by the application of pressure to the main arteries on either side of the neck. In a choke, pain is caused as pressure is applied to the front of the neck against the thorax and choking results. Although categorized as groundwork techniques, strangles and chokes (as with arm-locks) can be applied with equal effect from more upright or standing postures.

It is essential that Uke taps in submission the instant he begins to experience the full, dizzy effect of shime-waza. It is equally important that Tori simultaneously releases his grip. Failure to do either within three or four seconds can result in Uke losing con-

SHIME-WAZA
STRANGLE TECHNIQUES

sciousness. In time, experienced judoka come to learn not only of ways in which they can fight off the effects of shi-

me-waza for extended periods of time, but also numerous ways of escaping before the full effects are felt.

TSUKIKOMI-JIME *THRUSTING CHOKE*

SHIME-WAZA

Tsukikomi-jime can be applied when your are straddling your opponent, or when you are on your back with your opponent on top of you, or even from a standing posture as demonstrated here. Whatever the position, you must always be on the alert for your opponent countering with an arm-lock on your thrusting straight arm before your tsukikomi-jime becomes effective.

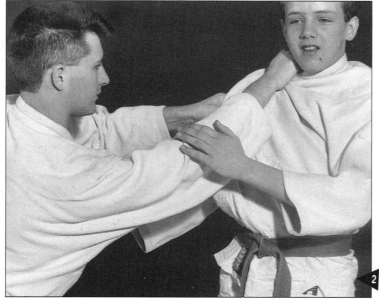

1 Tori has taken a palm-downwards grip of Uke's left top lapel, with his fingers on the inside of the jacket. Simultaneously Tori has grasped Uke's right lapel with his left hand, fingers outside and thumb inside the jacket.

2 To apply the technique Tori straightens his left arm. He leans forwards on it to thrust Uke's left lapel to the left across Uke's throat. At the same time Tori tightens the thrust by counter-pulling on Uke's right lapel.

Okuri-eri-jime can be a most effective technique as it applies pressure to your opponent's throat and the side of his neck at the same time. If necessary, you can increase the power of this technique by dropping to your rear and wrapping your legs around your opponent to help control his body movement.

1 Tori has reached his right hand over the right shoulder of the seated Uke and taken a deep grip high up on Uke's left lapel. Tori's thumb is on the inside of Uke's jacket and the bony edge of his right forearm is across Uke's throat. Tori's left arm has passed beneath Uke's left armpit and (with thumb inside) has grasped Uke's right lapel high up towards his own right forearm.

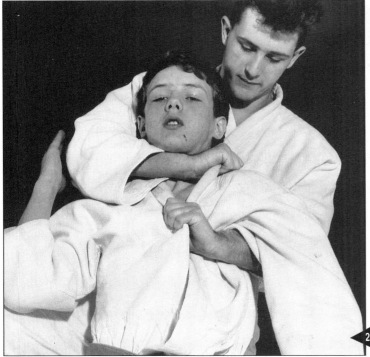

2 To apply the technique, Tori's right shoulder presses against the back of Uke's head. Then, leaning slightly backwards and pulling Uke with him, Tori presses into Uke's throat with his right forearm and pulls down hard on Uke's lapel with his left hand.

KATA-HA-JIME *SINGLE WING STRANGLE*

Kata-ha-jime, also called single wing choke, is generally demonstrated from a position in which you are on one knee behind your opponent, who is seated on the mat. Like most strangles or chokes, it can be applied equally from either right or left, but a normal right-handed attack is demonstrated here.

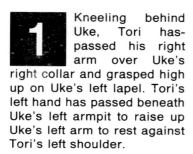 Kneeling behind Uke, Tori has passed his right arm over Uke's right collar and grasped high up on Uke's left lapel. Tori's left hand has passed beneath Uke's left armpit to raise up Uke's left arm to rest against Tori's left shoulder.

2 To apply the technique, Tori pushes his left hand past the back of Uke's head and rests it on the top of his own right forearm. He pulls on Uke's left lapel with his right hand and presses Uke's head forwards with his left hand in order to maximize pressure across the front of Uke's throat.

Hadake-jime, sometimes also referred to simply as naked strangle, is so called because no use is made of your opponent's jacket when applying the technique. It can be applied from the rear of your opponent in either a sitting or lying position, but generally he sits on the mat and you kneel behind for the purpose of demonstration.

1 From a kneeling position behind Uke, Tori has passed his right arm over Uke's right shoulder slipping the right forearm beneath Uke's chin and across the throat. Tori's right hand rests on the inside elbow of his bent left arm and the back of his left hand is positioned ready to apply pressure.

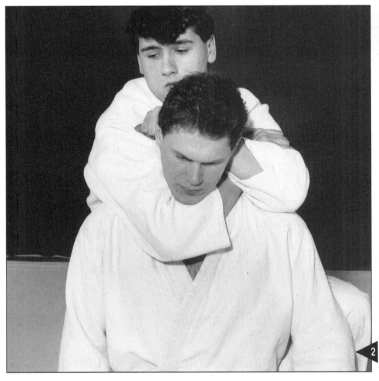

2 To apply the technique, Tori presses Uke's head forward with the back of his left hand and pulls across Uke's throat with his right forearm. This action becomes more effective as Tori leans slightly backwards and pulls Uke against his abdomen.

KATA-JUJI-JIME *HALF CROSS STRANGLE*

This is the first of three strangles which come under the general heading of juji-jime and which differ in the manner in which your hands take a grip on your opponent's collar. Nami-juji-jime and gyaku-juji-jime are the other two.

1 With his right palm upwards, Tori slides his fingers beneath Uke's right lapel to grasp Uke's collar by the right side of his neck. With his left palm facing downwards, Tori's left forearm crosses over his right forearm. Tori's left thumb slides deep inside the back of Uke's collar which is then gripped with his fingers on the outside.

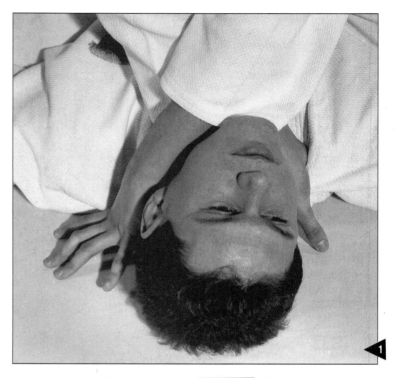

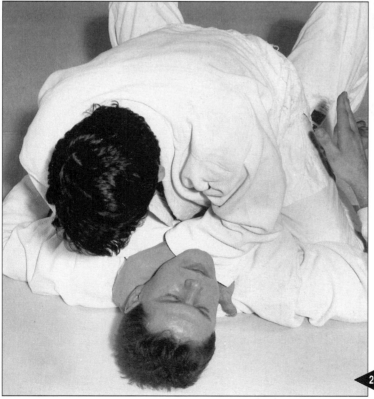

2 To apply the technique Tori leans his weight forward, screwing Uke's collar inwards on each side of the neck with a twisting grip. Pressure is applied to both sides of Uke's neck from Tori's wrists.

This technique is most effective if you can ensure that the outer bony edge of your forearm is pressed tightly against the front of your opponent's throat. If you attempt nami-juji-jime when you are on your back with an opponent above you, ensure that you control his body with your legs.

1 Tori's left arm crosses over his right and the thumbs of both hands slide in deep around Uke's collar, which is then gripped tightly with the fingers of both hands on the outside of the jacket.

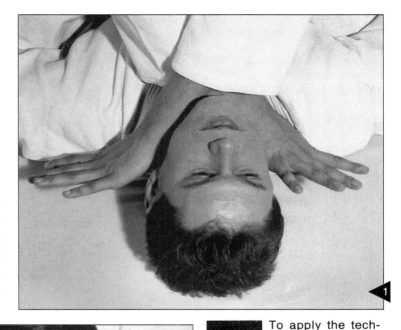

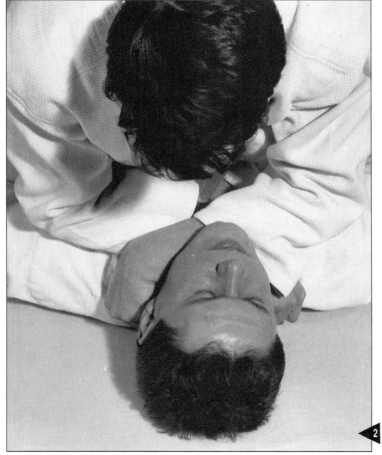

2 To apply the technique Tori leans forward and his elbows push outwards. The fist of each grip is twisted inwards so that the back of Tori's knuckles apply pressure to each side of Uke's neck.

SHIME-WAZA

The difference between gyaku-juji-jime and the other two juji-jime techniques is that here both your hands take a deep grip on your opponent's collar with both sets of fingers on the inside of the jacket.

1 With the palm facing upwards, Tori slides the fingers of his left hand deep into Uke's left-side collar and takes a grip with thumb on the outside of the jacket. Tori's right arm crosses over the left arm. Tori then slides the fingers of his right hand, also palm upwards, deep into Uke's right-side collar and takes a grip on the jacket with his thumb on the outside.

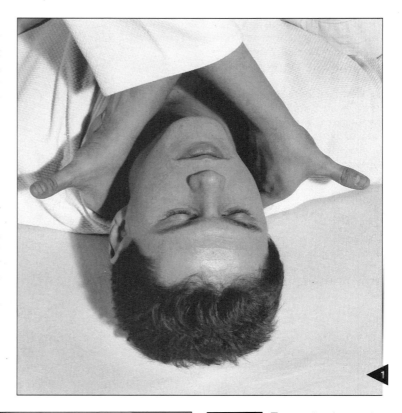

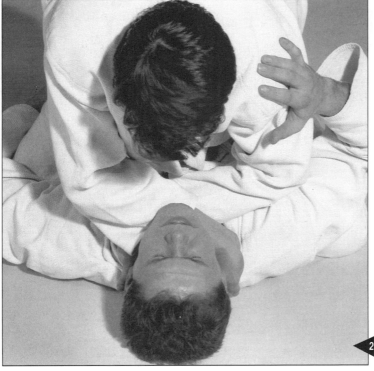

2 To apply the technique Tori leans his weight forwards and bends his arms out at the elbows. He tightens his grip by twisting each hand outwards so that the back of his hands press against the sides of Uke's neck.

Tomoe-jime can be applied from an upright standing or kneeling posture, with the opponents facing each other as demonstrated. This can be most useful in either randori or contests whenever you create circumstances in which your arm loops over the top of your opponent's head in order to apply the technique.

1 Tori (on the left) and Uke are each in a normal right-side posture as Tori, still grasping Uke's left lapel with his right hand, loops his right arm over Uke's head and carries the gripped lapel to Uke's right rear shoulder. Note that Tori's thumb remains inside Uke's jacket lapel, clenched fingers on the outside.

2 Simultaneously Tori releases Uke's right sleeve and passes his left arm over his right to grasp Uke's left lapel, fingers clenched inside and thumb outside, across the front of Uke's throat.

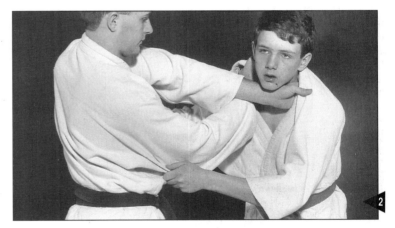

3 Tori bends his elbows to shorten his arms and applies the technique fully by twisting his clenched fists and tightening the grip in a scissor-type action. See how Uke releases his grip on Tori's right sleeve to tap clearly his submission.

WOMEN'S JUDO

Any references made in this book to 'him', 'his' or 'he' apply equally in Judo to the feminine gender as there is little or no sexism — or (thankfully!) any other '-ism' — in the sport. We are all judoka: players of every creed and colour, age and sex.

The small amount of sexism referred to above does exist (certainly within the British Judo Council's jurisdiction) in recognizing that however nimble, quick-thinking and skilful many women players might be, they are not as ideally equipped as the menfolk where strength and stamina are concerned. So, while men and women may sometimes participate in mixed randori and kata, they are separated in competitions and also in their syllabus work over and above the level of 3rd Kyu (green).

Beyond 3rd Kyu (green) a woman judoka must continue to learn and be able to demonstrate from the syllabus the same range of techniques as a man in order to progress to each higher grade. However, her contest ability will not, as with a man, be any part of the deciding factor in any promotion. Instead, she will be assessed more upon her style, posture and the performance of set demonstrations from ju-no-kata (page 135), which is a self-defence kata combining body control with supple movement.

This knowledge of ju-no-kata will be expected of her in addition to the gradually progressive knowledge she will have to acquire of nage-no-kate (which male judoka will be learning also in the normal course of their grading progress).

Thus, in order to qualify eventually for her black belt (1st Dan), a British Judo Council female judoka must be able to perform both nage-no-kata and ju-no-kata in full as well as the first fifteen techniques in katame-no-kata (formal groundwork). This is in addition to completing the normal syllabus work on all techniques. This British Judo Council policy places the emphasis in women's Judo particularly upon the theory and the knowledge of kata as a qualification for promotion to the higher grades.

Barbara Classens of West Germany beats Christine Cicot of France in the 1984 European Championships.

There is no standard age at which youngsters take up Judo, though the British Judo Council will not enrol members under six years of age. From six to nine years old, boys and girls are registered as Primary Grades and do not become fully fledged Junior Members until reaching the age of ten years.

At the age of sixteen, a Junior becomes a Senior Member, though there are Esquire Class competitions for which entry is restricted to male and female players between the ages of sixteen and eighteen. In terms of competitive Judo, this is a transitional stage which helps the immature young player to prepare for the much stronger opposition he or she is likely to meet among higher age groups.

Within a club, boys and girls train and practise as Juniors and even compete against each other in open competition. At this level there is often little difference between the abilities of the two sexes per age and weight groups. However, at more serious events outside the club there are separate contest categories for boys and girls. These are further broken down into age, weight or grade categories depending on the nature of the competition. Weight categories can begin from as low as under 20 kg and range upwards in 5 kg divisions to 65 kg and over, all depending on the size of the competition entry.

The lower age group (under-ten) Primary Grades soon respond to dojo disciplines, their interest often being stimulated by the introduction of Judo-based games and team competitions in addition to syllabus work on Judo techniques. These grades work through a syllabus very similar to that of the older players, but instead of achievement being marked by a change of belt colour their progress is indicated by a system of coloured bands, or tabs, which are affixed to the ends of their white belts. Primary Grades are usually examined and promoted within their own club.

Whatever length of time a youngster remains a Primary Grade, grade progress and ability is taken into account when he or she is eventually transferred to a Junior Mem-

A mixed class of juniors at practice.

JUNIOR JUDO

bership grade. British Judo Council Junior Membership begins at ten years of age with a white belt (6th Kyu) and moves upwards through yellow (5th Kyu) and orange (4th Kyu) to green (3rd Kyu). At each grade of 6th, 5th and 4th Kyu, the judoka's progress is marked with a series of three tabs of a colour the same as the next higher Kyu grade. These tabs are progressively awarded at examinations and affixed to the ends of the existing belts. The first tab is ichi, the second ni and the third san.

On reaching 3rd Kyu (green), a BJC Junior continues to attain ichi, ni and san tabs. The first three qualified for are blue, the second three are brown and the third set are black. No BJC Junior Member

ever receives a grade higher than 3rd Kyu (green), though the extent and colour of tabs will indicate the full degree of theoretical and practical abilities. There is no blue, brown or black belt award to BJC Junior members.

The BJC's policy is based upon their recognition of the difficult transition a Junior would experience in qualifying immediately for a comparable grade when transferring to Senior Membership at the age of sixteen. He or she would be required to defeat a line-up of Senior blue, brown or black belt grades and the likelihood of any Junior doing this would be very unlikely. Judo skills apart, there is generally a vast difference between the strength, stamina and experience of a sixteen-

A girl demonstrates her initiative and skill against a heavier boy opponent.

year-old and an adult judoka. Junior green belts usually transfer to the Senior ranks by qualifying as either green or blue belts, and if they are exceptional they soon make progress at subsequent Senior Grading examinations.

Junior players work to a syllabus similar to that of adults, though the duration of any contest work, after they have completed the rest of their periodic examinations, may be of only two minutes' duration. Some organizations also impose a restriction upon Junior judoka using arm-locks or strangle techniques during contests, and not all teach kata to any great extent.

JUDO KATA

We have seen how Judo as a sport includes throwing, hold-downs, arm-locks and strangles. Judo as a martial art form becomes complete with the study of kata (form, or demonstration) and includes the delivery of kicks, blows and other techniques too dangerous for inclusion in randori or any sort of sporting contest. The seven types of kata taught in Judo include:

Randori-no-kata, which is comprised of nage-no-kata (kata of throws) and katame-no-kata (kata of the ground).

Kime-no-kata, which teaches the art of attack and defence in actual combat situations.

Kodokan-goshin-jitsu, a kata made up of twenty-one self-defence techniques against both armed and unarmed opponents, which was only introduced to the Kodokan in 1958.

Ju-no-kata (kata of suppleness), a performance of gentle movements showing how to control the body in a self-defensive emergency and apply minimum energy against an opponent to maximum effect.

Itsutsu-no-kata, a combination of grace through movements which include some ju-jitsu techniques.

Koshiki-no-kata (kata of ancient forms), which combines the teaching of advanced techniques with a deep insight into the theory of Judo.

In each of the kata, a series of techniques are performed with a partner in a combination of grace and precision which can be seen at either demonstrations or kata championships held to determine the finest exponents of this skilful art.

The kata which most con-

With a student partner Sensei Caffary here demonstrates some of the countless kata movements which are performed with a grace and deliberate movement that at the same time manage to reveal their strength and power.

JUDO KATA

cern BJC Kyu grades up to 1st Dan are, or course, nage-no-kata, katame-no-kata and ju-no-kata. Most, if not all, of the techniques featured in each of the two first-mentioned programmes are demonstrated in this book as individual techniques. What cannot be explained within the extent of this book is the manner or form in which the techniques need to be performed in order to become a kata presentation. The procedure of linking together all the movements of each technique from beginning to end so that they provide a flowing, non-stop performance (or kata) is a ceremonial which must be learned separately.

The individual techniques and movements of ju-no-kata are dissimilar from almost all syllabus work and women judoka must study with their instructor in order to achieve black belt status under BJC regulations.

Not all Judo organizations demand a knowledge of kata as part of a judoka's qualification to progress. However, a proper study of kata will enhance the quality of your Judo, improve your concentration and tranquility and enlighten you further as to the true essence of the Gentle Way.

Nage-no-kata (kata of throws) comprises three techniques from each of five categories of throws. They are:

Te-waza (hand techniques)
Uki-otoshi (*floating drop*)
Ippon-seoi-nage (*one-arm shoulder throw*)
Kata-guruma (*shoulder wheel*)

Koshi-waza (hip techniques)
Uki-goshi (*floating hip throw*)
Harai-goshi (*sweeping loin throw*)
Tsuri-komi-goshi (*resisting hip throw*)

Ashi-waza (leg and foot techniques)
Okuri-ashi-barai (*side sweeping ankle*)
Sasae-tsurikomi-ashi (*propping drawing ankle*)
Uchi-mata (*inner thigh*)

Ma-sutemi-waza (rear sacrifice techniques)
Tomoe-nage (*stomach throw*)
Ura-nage (*rear throw*)
Sumi-gaeshi (*corner throw*)

Yoko-sutemi-waza (side sacrifice techniques)
Yoko-gake (*side dash*)
Yoko-guruma (*side wheel*)
Uki-waza (*floating throw*)

Katame-no-kata (kata of the ground) comprises five techniques from each of three categories. They are:

Osae-komi-waza (hold down techniques)
Kuzure-kesa-gatame (*scarf hold*)
Kata-gatame (*shoulder hold*)
Kami-shiho-gatame (*upper four quarter hold*)
Yoko-shiho-gatame (*side four quarter hold*)
Kuzure-kami-shiho-gatame (*broken upper four quarter hold*)

Shime-waza (strangle techniques)
Kata-juji-jime (*half cross strangle*)
Hadake-jime (*naked choke lock*)
Okuri-eri-jime (*sliding collar lock*)
Kata-ha-jime (*single wing lock*)
Gyaku-juji-jime (*reverse cross lock*)

Kansetsu-waza (arm-locks)
Ude-garami (*entangled arm-lock*)
Juji-gatame (*cross arm-lock*)
Ude-gatame (*arm crush*)
Hiza-gatame (*knee arm-lock*)
Ashi-garami (*leg arm-lock*)

GRADINGS AND SYLLABUS

To whichever body or association any individual or club is related, a judoka's progress in Judo is marked by the award of differently coloured belts at each stage of proficiency, the colour depending upon the standard of results achieved at periodic examinations.

All judoka begin as Kyu (class) grades. The Kyu grades and their belt colours range upwards from 6th Kyu (white), to 5th Kyu (yellow), 4th Kyu (orange), 3rd Kyu (green), 2nd Kyu (blue) and 1st Kyu (brown).

After 1st Kyu, a brown belt will strive for his black belt (1st Dan). Later, examination successes and seniority may take him or her progressively through 2nd, 3rd, 4th and 5th Dan grades. Beyond that, 6th, 7th and 8th Dans wear red-and-white striped belts. Ninth and 10th Dans wear all-red belts.

The examinations at which players perform to improve their Kyu and Dan grades are called 'gradings'. These are held once every three or four months at varying times in all local areas. From 6th Kyu (white) up to and including 3rd Kyu (green), BJC examiners tend to pay more attention to the knowledge of theory and demonstration of the syllabus than to the outcome of any contest in which the judoka might be expected to take part. On the other hand, 3rd Kyu (green) are expected to begin showing signs of familiarity with the early stages of kata, in addition to their knowledge of syllabus work relative to their particular stage of progress and qualification.

In overall terms a syllabus is a structure of techniques which, between 6th Kyu (white) and 1st Dan (black), should take the student progressively through all nage-waza (throwing techniques) contained in the original gokyo-no-waza as well as groups from each of osae-komi-waza (hold-down techniques), shime-waza (strangle techniques) and kansetsu-waza (arm-locks) which are all part of katame-waza (groundwork techniques). All of these you will find within the pages of this book, though quite deliberately they have not been presented in a syllabus format as the order of presentation differs from one Judo governing body to another.

It should be remembered that British Judo Council examiners at gradings refer to the names of individual techniques in Japanese when asking students to demonstrate. Points are deducted from students who fail to understand and require to be given the English name.

An additional requirement of the British Judo Council is for an aspiring 2nd Kyu (blue belt) to be able to provide a demonstration of the first three movements (both left- and right-hand techniques) in nage-no-kata; the second six with both left- and right-hand techniques as well as the first five of katame-no-kata when he tries for 1st Kyu (brown); and when trying for his 1st Dan (black) a judoka must, apart from his contest work, demonstrate nage-no-kata complete with both left- and right-hand techniques and the second five of katame-no-kata. All these kata techniques are displayed individually in this book, but see page 135 to find out just what form the kata itself takes on.

The way in which the syllabus and grading procedure for women above 3rd Kyu (green) can differ from that of men is explained on page 132.

CONTESTS

An official contest area comprises a mat measuring 9 m square surrounded by a clearly marked 1 m danger area which is further surrounded by a safety area of 3 m width. It is in such an area (possibly smaller for Juniors or for tournaments which are not so important) that a judoka will compete and display all his or her acquired skills in combat. The rules and regulations under which contests take place may differ slightly according to the organizers, and the occasion may vary in importance depending on whether it is a club-level competition, an area Grading Examination contest or an official championship.

Unlike boxing or wrestling, a Judo contest is not fought over a number of 'rounds'. It is fought over a limited period of time which can vary from two or three minutes to six minutes or longer, depending upon the status or requirements of the organizers. The contest is controlled by a referee and two corner judges, the referee signalling scores to the off-mat table where sit a scorer (recorder) and timekeeper.

The contestants are referred to as 'red' and 'white', the 'red' competitor generally wearing a red belt or a red ribbon tied on to the back of the normal belt. The scoreboard on the table facing the mat is half-red and half-white, each half recording the scores of each contestant.

The referee scores ippon (a full ten points) in favour of the contestant who performs a perfect throw, holds an opponent down in osae-komi for an agreed period of time (usually thirty seconds) or achieves a submission from the application of an arm-lock or a strangle. A contest ends immediately in favour of the contestant scoring ippon.

The referee scores waza-ari (seven points) in favour of the contestant who throws well but not so perfectly as to warrant a full ippon. Waza-ari is also awarded for being able to hold an opponent down for only twenty-five seconds, not the full thirty seconds.

Lesser awards of yuko (five points) and koka (three points) are given in respect of less proficient performances.

Penalty points are awarded for various rule infringements: shido (three points) for a minor breach of rules; chui (five points) for a repeated minor offence or major infringement; and keikoku (seven points) for a repeated minor offence or a serious infringement. Hansoku-make is a ten-point penalty awarded against a contestant who repeats an infringement or commits a grave infringement of the rules, and in such a case the recipient is disqualified and loses the contest.

Rules which must not be infringed upon include all the 'dos' and 'don'ts' you have come across elsewhere in this book. In a contest situation there are additional prohibitions such as deliberately moving outside the contest area, employing dangerous or unlawful techniques or even talking (whether your language is good or bad).

Competitors should study a full book of rules and watch a referee and corner judges at work at an official tournament.

The referee communicates with the scorer during a contest by calling out the points or penalties awarded to each 'red' or 'white' contestant and simultaneously signalling with certain arm movements. Should a contest not be decided by a clear ippon, the winner is the contestant with most points after penalties have been taken in to consideration. Sometimes these amount to hantei (equal points) and in such a case the referee awards hikiwake (a draw) or yusei-gachi (a win by superiority) if he considers the latter to be clear in his estimation.

Of course, there is much more detail attached to refereeing a contest and to deciding who has won or lost or why. When things do happen during a Judo contest, they happen quickly — often more quickly than the eye can see — and the uninitiated can rarely understand why a decision has gone this or that way. This is perhaps the reason why Judo has never managed to become a popular spectator sport. On the other hand, devotees can sit for hours on end enjoying the spectacle of Judo skills.

CONTESTS

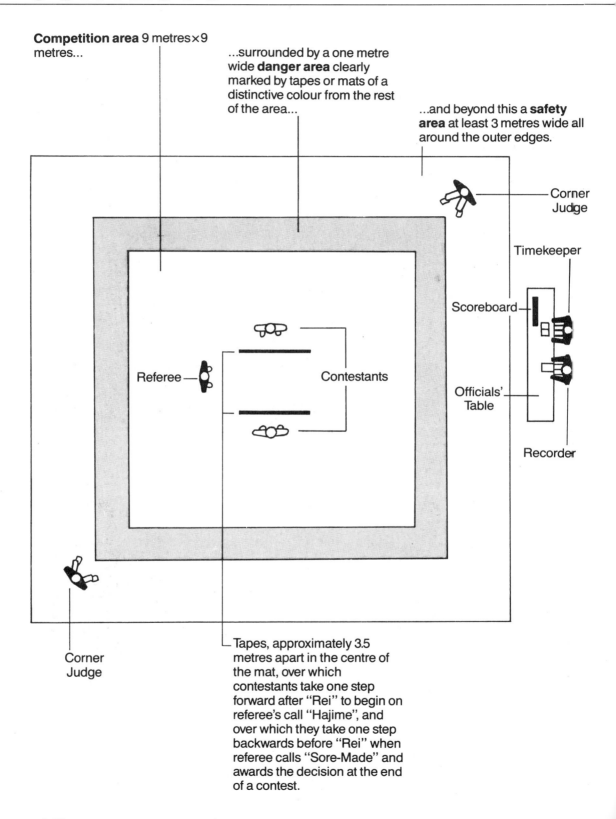

Competition area 9 metres×9 metres...

...surrounded by a one metre wide **danger area** clearly marked by tapes or mats of a distinctive colour from the rest of the area...

...and beyond this a **safety area** at least 3 metres wide all around the outer edges.

Corner Judge

Timekeeper

Scoreboard

Referee

Contestants

Officials' Table

Recorder

Corner Judge

Tapes, approximately 3.5 metres apart in the centre of the mat, over which contestants take one step forward after "Rei" to begin on referee's call "Hajime", and over which they take one step backwards before "Rei" when referee calls "Sore-Made" and awards the decision at the end of a contest.

REFEREES' SIGNALS

 Ippon
Outstretched arm is raised upwards with palm facing timekeeper as referee calls "Ippon" to signify award of 10 points, followed by the call of "Sore Made" to signify "That is all", or end of the contest.

▲ **Rei**
On referee's command "Rei", opponents exchange standing bows and take one stop forward towards each other.

▼ **Wazari**
Outstretched arm is raised sideways to shoulder height, palm facing down, as referee calls "Wazari" to signify the award of 7 points.

▲ **Hajime**
The referee calls "Hajime" to signal either the start of a contest or resumption after a stoppage. There are no arm movements for this command.

Yuko ▶
Outstretched arm is raised to 45 degrees up from side of body, palm down, as referee calls "Yoko" to signify award of 5 points.

REFEREES' SIGNALS

▼ Wazari-Awasete-Ippon
Arm raised as for Ippon as referee calls "Wazari-Awasete-Ippon" to signify 10 points resulting from two cumulative Wazari scores by one opponent, followed by the call of "Sore Made" to signify end of the contest.

▲ Koka
Forearm only is raised with palm of hand facing forward at shoulder height as referee calls "Koka" to signify the award of 3 points.

Wazari-No-Muko ▶
Arm outstretched above head, palm facing inwards and waived from side-to-side as referee calls "Wazari-no-Muko" to indicate that a particular technique is not valid.

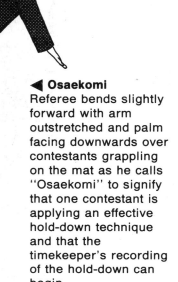

◀ Osaekomi
Referee bends slightly forward with arm outstretched and palm facing downwards over contestants grappling on the mat as he calls "Osaekomi" to signify that one contestant is applying an effective hold-down technique and that the timekeeper's recording of the hold-down can begin.

◀ Osaekomi-Toketa
Referee straightens up from Osaekomi posture and moves outstretched arm left-to-right over contestants as he calls "Osaekomi-Toketa" to signify the hold-down has been broken and the timing of it must immediately cease.

REFEREES' SIGNALS

▼ **Yoshi**
Referee removes hands from Sono-Mama posture and in this instance calls "Yoshi" to indicate that action may be resumed.

▲ **Sono-Mama**
Referee places an outstretched palm on each contestant and calls "Sono-Mama" to indicate they must stop action immediately but 'freeze' and remain exactly as they are locked together. During Sono-Mama the players can be either instructed, lifted bodily to safety, or penalised if either has commited an offence.

▲ **Kogeki-Seyo**
Referee raises hands to chest height, arms across chest with palms outstretched and rotates forearms whilst facing player from whom more action is required.

◄ **Jikan**
Arm outstretched forward from shoulder with palm facing timekeeper as referee calls "Jikan" as signal for the timekeeper's clock to be stopped for time out.

Hantei ▶
Referee holds outstretched right arm above head, palm facing inwards, and calls "Hantei" at end of a contest to indicate the need for consultation with the two corner judges about a contest ending with equal score.

REFEREES' SIGNALS

◀ **Shosha**
The movement the referee makes by raising either arm to 45 degrees above shoulder height, with palm facing upwards, in the direction of whichever contestant is declared the winner at the end of the contest. If this comes after Hantei, and the decision is not Hike-Wake, the referee will call ''Yusei-gachi'' (win by superiority) if that is the majority decision made between himself and the two judges.

▲ **Hike-Wake**
The right forearm is raised and lowered to waist level (with palm facing inward) as the referee calls ''Hike-Wake'' to signify a draw at the end of a contest.

Any stoppage in a contest arising out of the referee having called ''Matte'' shall be taken out of the time limit for the contest.

The command ''Matte'' (or ''Wait') is pronounced ''Mattay''.

Unless shown otherwise, a referee generally gives all signals with his right arm or hand.

When signalling points or penalties, a referee also calls out ''Red'' or ''White'' to indicate to the recorder on the officials' table which player is the recipient.

A referee may temporarily halt a contest at any time by calling ''Matte'' for which there is no hand signal. ''Matte'' (or ''Wait'') is called when any accident or difficulty occurs (such as an injury), or there is the need for a player to adjust his judogi when a player has stepped outside of the contest area, when a prohibited act has been committed, or when contestants in groundwork have virtually come to a stalemate situation, or for whatever other reason the referee deems that a stoppage is necessary.

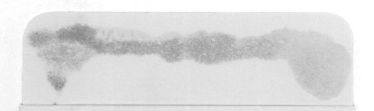